EVERYWOMAN'S MONEY™

Less Debt, More Cash

by Avis Pohl

alpha books
201 West 103rd Street
Indianapolis, IN 46290

A Pearson Education Company

International Standard Book Number: 0-02-864011-X
Library of Congress Catalog Card Number: Available from the Library of Congress.

03   02   01   8   7   6   5   4   3   2   1

Interpretation of the printing code: The rightmost number of the first series of numbers is the year of the book's printing; the rightmost number of the second series of numbers is the number of the book's printing. For example, a printing code of 01-1 shows that the first printing occurred in 2001.

Printed in the United States of America

ALPHA BOOKS

PUBLISHER:
Marie Butler-Knight

PRODUCT MANAGER:
Phil Kitchel

MANAGING EDITOR:
Jennifer Chisholm

ACQUISITIONS EDITOR:
Mike Sanders

DEVELOPMENT EDITOR:
Nancy Warner

PRODUCTION EDITORS:
JoAnna Kremer
Christy Wagner

COVER DESIGNER:
Anne Jones

BOOK DESIGNER:
Trina Wurst

INDEXER:
Amy Lawrence

LAYOUT/PROOFREADING:
Mary Hunt
Lizbeth Patterson

EVERYWOMAN'S COMPANY

EXECUTIVE PROJECT DIRECTOR:
Jan Black

MANAGING PROJECT DIRECTOR:
Joseph Roberts

CONTRIBUTING EDITOR:
Diana Williams

Contents

Foreword

The *Everywoman's Money*™ series is one more expression of the Everywoman vision to educate and empower women to fund the lives they want to live, and to create and sustain financial well-being. These books, and all other Everywoman's Money™ products and events, are rooted in this mission.

Through the creation and presentation of the Everywoman's Money™ Conferences around the country, women are telling us what they want to know and how they want it explained. Women know their need to be money-smart is more essential than ever. They are emerging with new levels of assets, responsibilities, and opportunities, requiring them to have a thorough knowledge of how money works.

Just as they are experiencing new opportunities, women also continue to be challenged by some very real financial risks. At this writing, two thirds of America's poor are women, many of whom lived middle-class lives until a divorce or death of a husband sent them into poverty. Eighty-five percent of the elderly poor are women, and 100,000 of the 127,000 people over 100 years of age are, you guessed it, women. Collectively, women still earn only 75 percent of what men earn, and their in-and-out careers (because of caring for children and parents) produce smaller pensions. In other words, women in general have less money available than men to sustain a life that lasts longer than men's.

Women must compensate for this shortfall by getting smart about money and how it grows so they can have enough for long enough. This is why Everywoman's Money™ exists. It is why we are committed to "teaching money like it's never been taught before."

Jan Black
Jody Temple-White

Founders, The Everywoman's Company and Project Green Purse

Introduction

The first time I visited my daughter in Seattle, she invited some of her friends for an informal supper to meet her mom. Since I am a financial planner, the young women picked my brain on the financial issues in their lives, and this became my first focus group for women.

Over the next few years my visits to Seattle included other suppers, meeting with Cena's friends one-on-one, and answering lots of e-mail messages. The over-riding topic was often debt, usually credit card debt and college loans. They wanted to learn to become debt-free enough to make goals for graduate school, owning a home, or having a newer car or a better apartment.

It has been such joy to receive e-mails and handwritten thank-you notes from these women as they have worked through their own financial problems and successes. Many of them have asked me to put my advice into a self-help book to share with other women like them.

Some of the stories in this book are from these women, their friends, and some of their mothers. I feel that part of this book was written for you by them. Thanks to the power of e-mail, Cena and I sent out messages asking for real-life concerns and success stories about working through debt discovery to recovery and on to successful financial management. The response was overwhelming, and I thank the following women who shared their stories so that my readers might benefit from their experiences: Debi Clark, Kathleen Witzak, Aicha Menedez, Alizabeth Fritz, Cena Pohl, Julie Hazle, Leslie Coven, Lisa H., Lisa Rojay, Mary deBaca, Monica deBaca, Patti Purdy, Sandy Kinney, Tara Brett, Thea McCue, Renee Weiler, Rosemary Flores, Louise Corley, and Rita Berger.

The content of the *Everywoman's Money: Less Debt, More Cash* takes the reader step-by-step from recognizing where she stands financially—whether or not more money is going out each month than is coming in—to finding out where her money is going. She can follow a step-by-step guide to develop a spending plan that will allow her to pay off her loans and then use the available cash to invest for future goals.

I hope that *Everywoman's Money: Less Debt, More Cash* will be a resource book and that you will actually write out the exercises. The journals you write at the end of each chapter should be re-visited periodically so that as your life experiences change, you will use these chapters to help you make appropriate financial decisions.

How This Book Is Organized

True to the *Everywoman's Money*™ brand, these books, and those that will follow, address specific financial topics with a particular personality and holistic tone that is smart, respectful, punchy, and warm.

Each *Everywoman's Money*™ book is organized to include:

Everywoman Stories

When you attend an Everywoman's Money™ Conference, you will meet Everywomen whose stories are told on video periodically throughout the day. Each chapter of these books opens with similar stories of real women. You will learn from them and apply their experiences to your own.

Coaching Tip

Karen Sheridan, our Everywoman's Money™ Coach at live events, is also your financial coach in these books. Karen is beloved for her frankness, humor, and passion for helping women like you master money. She owns her own money-management company in the Northwest.

Money Therapy

Olivia Mellan, Money Therapist and popular speaker at Everywoman's Money™ events, accompanies you as you read the books through an ongoing commentary called "Money Therapy." Olivia presents the psychology side of money. She is noted for her groundbreaking work in identifying money personalities.

Reader's Journal and Assessments

For readers who want to record what they have learned and the steps they want to take, there are journal entry pages at the end of each chapter. Throughout the books, there are also places for the reader to complete helpful financial assessments and information.

Glossary

A glossary of terms related to the title of each book is included to help you talk the topic.

Acknowledgments

I thank Jan Black, founder of the Everywoman's Company, for giving me the opportunity to write *Everywoman's Money: Less Debt, More Cash* as part of the first series of money books dedicated to women. I appreciate Diana Williams for the contribution she has made to researching facts and developing the glossary and Karen Sheridan and Olivia Mellan for their additions to the text.

Some good advice has been contributed by my accountant, Brad Borncamp, CPA; money therapist, Olivia Mellan; and money coach, Karen Sheridan.

Thank you to Mike Sanders, Nancy Warner, JoAnna Kremer, and Christy Wagner at Alpha Books, who brought this book forward. Thank you to Dee Lee and Deborah Owens for being there throughout this project. And I especially thank Joe Roberts, whose continuous support and encouragement have helped me to make this finished product available to you.

Avis L. Pohl

Trademarks

C eleste (Baltimore, Maryland) was the first to make fun of the way she avoided managing her money. Everyone close to her knew that she had a keen distaste for keeping her check register current, her purse organized, and her spending planned. She often forgot where she placed bills, and it was a red-letter day when she could actually find a receipt for an item she wanted to return. She wasn't irresponsible. In fact, she was a highly successful department store manager with a well-known upscale clothing chain. At work, others kept track of data. Celeste only had to review it. At home, however, it was a different story. Celeste was on her own, and she was anything but effective.

The truth is, Celeste is a bright, creative woman with a deep capacity for managing her money. So what was the problem? She simply dreaded the boredom of having to fit into what she regarded as the "stale old tradition" of money management. She had tried it many times and failed to maintain the momentum, and then finally tossed the ledgers and her hopes of getting it together financially.

Seated next to Celeste on a plane ride to Dallas from Baltimore sat Patricia, an ad exec turned stay-at-home mom. Celeste dozed and when she woke up, Patricia was opening a small, bright pouch. Inside were stamped envelopes, a checkbook, a pen, and a list of bills to be paid. Celeste shifted in her seat, not liking the image because it reminded her that her bills were at home, unopened and scattered.

Patricia caught Celeste's glance and said, "It's my way of getting it done when and where I can." Celeste quipped, "Yeah? Well, whatever works." The words triggered an insight as she said them. "Whatever works." Celeste suddenly wanted to know what else Patricia did to manage her money her way, and by the time they reached Dallas, Celeste was a convert to a new way of handling money. The new way would be her way.

She vowed to become responsible about organizing her money, and at the same time promised herself she would find a way to do it that was self-motivating. She promised herself success, not another failure. The first thing she did was make a new rule: no more self-demeaning jokes about her money management. The second thing she did was write, "Money, my way" on a small paper and tape it to her mirror. Celeste moved slowly but steadily into a new pattern of behavior built on her revised belief that she could do it. She bucked tradition and created her own.

Chapter 1

Finding Your Way to Less Debt and More Cash

The Bottom Line

It doesn't matter if the way you manage your money is considered "different," so long as you find a way that works for you, and stick to it.

We now live in a customized world. Have you noticed? It has been sneaking up on us for a couple of decades. Gone are the days when companies mass-produced and pushed products out to customers as if we were identical buying units.

Not anymore. Instead, the world out there is ready and eager to bend, mold, and shape itself to your needs. You can now buy a car with seats that accommodate your height, spinal curve, and body temperature. You can order a doll to match the same features as the child who will play with it. You can monogram just about anything in your house from sports bags to mailboxes. Think about it. You can even create your own personal makeup.

And, the same applies to your own money management systems. The first order of business in creating one for yourself is to think about customization. What fits you best?

What's You?

Let's go through that again. It used to be that "one size should fit all" because one method was the best. We've all seen the typical stereotype of the most "recommended" money management system. It was— picture this—a person bent over an oversized leather-bound ledger. That book probably had pages that were lined and we can bet they were colored light green. Receipts don't clutter the picture. They were carefully bound up in bundles with rubber bands and stored away in file drawers.

Of course, there was also the other financial management system, but it was "the bad one." It was a shoebox. That shoebox was the place people tossed receipts, warranties, insurance policies, unopened mail, gum wrappers, and who knows what else. On April 14, they were all dumped on some poor tax accountant's desk.

These stereotypes haunt us because they make us feel worlds of guilt. Managing money is serious leather-bound business; we are supposed to be perfectly organized; we must be scrupulous about records and details; we must be conscientious, knowledgeable, detailed, thorough, and complete. Well … lose the stereotypes and myths.

Holding on to a myth about what a money management system is "supposed" to be does not work. It actually prevents a person from being personally effective. Fighting off the guilt takes energy away from creating a system that does work. So, turn down the volume and let's get on with the real task, which is designing a system that is customized for you.

The Range of Possibilities

First, let's be sure we understand the range of possibilities with money management systems. Think of three people you know and describe what you can of their money management systems and how they generally get things done. Here are a few examples:

Example #1: LynnDee uses her dining room table a lot. It is the first stop as she walks into her house. She unloads the mail there. Her checkbook is always there. She seems to like to spread out. Sitting at the table, you can see her oversized wall calendar on a kitchen wall. It is covered with written notes. The tackboard next to it is covered with pinned-up notices, invitations, notes, announcements, and newsletters. LynnDee is a very artistic person. Her house is a flood of color and filled with framed art, stenciling, and stylish antiques. I also happen to know that her drawers are in chaos, often spilling their contents when pulled open.

Example #2: Sally works as the photographer and librarian for an architectural firm. Beautifully dressed, Sally is famous among her women friends for storing her off-season wardrobe at the cleaners. She says her closets are too small and this way everything is cleaned and ready when the season rolls around again. She keeps a small set of in-between clothes at home for the variable spring and fall weather. Sally was also an early bird in using the computer to print out household bill payments. She got a box of checks that would work with her printer. She programmed it so that the monthly bills only require the dollar amount to be keyed in. She even bought window envelopes and had the recipient's address printed on the check, which can then show in the window. Her friends had a load of fun with that one.

Example #3: Marge loves to play sports and coach her kids on their teams. She is always on the move and either lives out of a gym bag, a locker at the community pool, or the trunk of her car. She carries all kinds of regalia with her wherever she goes: water, pocketknife, change of clothes, deodorant, flashlight, address book, and checkbook. She lives in bits and pieces, here and there, except when she's in a workout or at a game. She puts her bills in one of those accordion files and carries it with her. She will pull it out and write some checks if she has a moment before the game, just sitting in the bleachers. Periodically, she takes the remaining stack of papers and files them in a drawer in her bedroom desk.

Think about your examples, or these three women. It doesn't take much to realize they are very different. Each has a lot of talent—but it is distinctive. They have strengths, but they aren't the same. Now just imagine trying to make them all follow the same process, methodology, or system in managing their money. Forget about it.

Quickly list some words to describe each or all of these women. Responsible, energetic, scheduled, visual, modular, colorful, systematic, portable, technical, thorough, flexible, busy, sporadic, persistent, and so on.

In short, each woman manages her money effectively, but each does it in a dramatically different way according to her own lifestyle and personality. The challenge is to identify what works for you, and how that can help you define your own effective money management system.

There are numerous so-called self-discovery instruments available these days to help you describe your individuality. Have you taken any? We can take tests that help us identify our learning styles (such as visual, kinesthetic, audio), our emotional intelligences, our colors (autumn, winter, spring, summer), and our personality styles (ISTJ, ENFP, and so on).

Whenever possible, it is fun and useful to fill out these questionnaires or take such tests. They are not diagnostic tests; instead, they are descriptive. They don't analyze a personality. Rather, they give you another way to describe yourself. And that is useful.

Whether you have taken such tests, now is the time to reflect upon and use any information you have about your profile. Let's do it by focusing on some categories that particularly relate to money management. We will talk through these categories and then brainstorm ways in which your particular traits can play out usefully in your money management system.

These categories are as follows:

❖ Timing
❖ Trappings
❖ Technology
❖ Tenacity
❖ Terms
❖ Triggers
❖ Trust Test
❖ Torpedoes

Timing

How do you relate to time? Are you intensely time-conscious? Are you methodical or sporadic? Does your adrenaline only kick in at the last minute? Do you enjoy performing under deadlines? Do you hate it? Do you do things in their good time? Is that boring or reassuring or rewarding?

Money is time. Time is money. A money management system must accommodate timing *or* the cost of ignoring timing. How you fashion your system has to mesh your sense of timing with the costs of time. You can certainly be sporadic or ignore deadlines. But it will probably cost you money.

There are dozens of ways of coping with the way we relate to timing. What keeps you on top of a schedule the easiest?

- ❑ Wall calendars
- ❑ Refrigerator lists
- ❑ Day timers
- ❑ Tickler files
- ❑ Alarms
- ❑ Reminder service
- ❑ Computer calendars
- ❑ Wireless organizer
- ❑ Other

What chunks of time work best for you?

- ❑ Monthly
- ❑ Weekly
- ❑ Daily

Ask people for their trade secrets. You might be surprised how much they will tell you.

Kathy writes a check the minute a bill arrives. Literally, she stands at her kitchen counter before she takes off her coat at night, reads her bills, and writes the checks. She stamps the envelope and then notes the day it is due for mailing. She keeps those letters in a chronological stack at the door and checks daily for which ones she should stick in the mailbox as she walks out in the morning to go to work.

Monica has just bought a calendar box. This is a rectangular box with 31 slots in it, numbered for the days of the month. She loves it. In those slots go bills according to their due date, tickets for the theater, auto inspection notices. All she does is keep an eye on the four or five days in front of her.

Trappings

Office Depot, Levingers, Hold Everything, and others are building corporate empires off *trappings*. The technical definition of money management system trappings is "stuff that is useful if you use it."

We all know trappings. We walk down aisles looking at them. There are colored folders coordinated with colored hanging files coordinated with colored labels. There are calculators that look like baubles with fake jewels for buttons or sturdy, no nonsense, financial calculators.

There are file cabinets that look like prison industry products and file cabinets that sport Chinese wood carvings. There are wall safes, fake book safes, and peach crates.

We can get distracted and disappointed by the trappings, believing they will solve problems they actually were never meant to solve. On the other hand, we can also find them to be enormously helpful, even inspiring. Again, think of their purpose and your needs.

Trappings can be …

- ❖ Motivators—they entice you to get to the task at hand.
- ❖ Organizers—they help sort, store, retrieve.
- ❖ Schedulers—they discipline the order of the tasks.
- ❖ Communicators—they can speed the movement of information.

Monica (remember her?) finds that beautiful pens just cry out to her to be held and used. She has a number of fountain pens that are cradled in a special felt-lined case on her desk. She genuinely likes to sit down, open that box, choose a pen, feel its weight, and admire its shine. She simply loves to write with it. She used to be a calligrapher, and this is her small way of remembering that art class. Doing bills is a chance to write and get off the computer. She adorns her files with scrolls and scripts, enjoying the simple pleasure of pen and ink.

Marcia, on the other hand, is a box person. She has a couple of sets of Shaker nesting boxes in which she stores paid bills and receipts.

She stores unpaid bills in a decorated cardboard box her son made in second grade.

What trappings motivate you?

Technology

Ever since the day the abacus was invented, we have searched for better technologies with which to run our numbers. And we're getting close to nirvana.

Computers are astoundingly helpful tools if a person puts in the investment and patience of loading and learning the software. A really helpful feature of technology is that you can load reminders, ticklers, screensavers, and icons. All of these allow you to customize the information and the formats so that they work for you.

Of course, low tech still works. Pencil and paper and a calculator (or not) keep you very close to your money as you enter each figure with your own hand. There can be something very relaxing about entering figures and writing checks.

Which tech works for you? What tools do you prefer?

Coaching Tip

One of the greatest things I ever did for myself was start writing "Thank you" on the bottom of my checks. I began this habit during a time when I was starting my business, a fearful time financially. Expressing thanks in this way caused me to stay in a place of gratitude instead of fear. I was grateful for the heat in my house, for the insurance coverage, for the computer repairman, and this habit conveyed it to them in a way that encouraged me, too. I recommend you try it.

Tenacity

The saying goes that no one can escape death or taxes. This is a useful idea because it turns us to the issue of our tenacity. Erin Brockovich, a frequent keynote speaker at the Everywoman's Money™ Conferences, says "stick-to-it-iveness" was her greatest lesson as a child. When it comes to less debt and more cash, we're in it for the long haul. The system you create for yourself will flex with you over the years.

A money management system requires some loyalty. If you decide to use a rolodex, then use it and forget the Microsoft Outlook list. At the same time, a system that doesn't work for you anymore needs to be revolutionized. In this case, be brave and go forward with something better. Upgrade.

What money management process can you be loyal to right now?

Terms

It is important at this point to ask yourself about the terms you will use to structure and sort your system. Adopt simple rules and stick to them, such as ...

❖ Last in, first out.

❖ Throw away what isn't relevant. Shed all extraneous paper that comes with bills at the moment you open them.

❖ April 16 is moving day. Every April, after taxes, move all last year's files to an archive place. Work only with the current year's files.

❖ Go automatic. Help yourself save and invest and even pay bills by doing as much of it as possible automatically through direct deposit and automatic bill paying.

What rules will you live by?

Triggers

Build triggers into your money system to help keep your batteries charged. Some ideas follow:

❖ Set a date to do bills each month. Keep it and reward yourself. Miss it and deny yourself.

❖ Partner with a friend to call or e-mail each other on the twentieth of each month, like a wake-up call.

❖ Display a picture of something or someone that motivates you to upgrade your money behavior.

What will trigger your positive money habits?

Trust Test

Do you trust your system? It is no good to put together a system based on someone's recommendations or tricks or hints if it doesn't work for you, or if you can't trust it. So keep working with your system until you have the faith that it's right for the way you personally process and organize information.

List the elements of how you currently manage your money (pay and organize your bills, save and invest, keep on top of what your money is doing, meet with your advisor[s]). Circle the elements that fit your style, cross out those that don't. Then think of alternatives for those you crossed off the list.

What does and doesn't work for you now?

Torpedoes

Finally, any system needs to pay attention to what can sabotage it. Know where your torpedoes are and what is firing them so you can win the war.

Some possible torpedoes include the following:

- ❖ A system that is too time-consuming and complex. Keep it simple.
- ❖ A system that is built on someone else's personality, not yours.
- ❖ A system that demands too much, too soon.
- ❖ A plan that doesn't include built-in rewards for the new behavior.

What torpedoes do you need to intercept in your money management system?

Your Money Personality

As you customize your plan, it is helpful for you to know your money personality. You have at least one, and probably a blend of two; this section will describe many of them.

There is great value in knowing what your money personality is so you can understand your behavior with money. It can also lead you to know how to counteract the resistance you may face as you upgrade your less-debt, more-cash position. For example, if you are a hoarder, you are going to naturally resist investing. Knowing this about yourself before you begin investing will prepare you to counteract the feelings.

Read the following descriptions of money personalities created by noted psychotherapist Olivia Mellan, author of *Money Harmony: Resolving Money Conflicts in Your Life and Relationships* (Walker & Company, 1995).

Hoarders hate to spend money on immediate pleasure purchases. They love to budget, plan, prioritize, and delay gratification for future fulfillment. To them, money is Security with a capital S. When it comes to spending and debt, hoarders tend to have no debt. They hate it when their mates rack up any debt, and tend to feel judgmental about any present purchase that compromises their or their family's "hoarding," such as nest eggs or emergency money.

Spenders love to spend money on immediate pleasure purchases. They hate to budget (hate the word "budget"—it makes them feel claustrophobic, deprived), and they can always think of something they'd like to spend their money on. They tend to be in debt, to live on the edge, and to juggle bill-paying. If they have to say "no" to themselves or put off buying something they want, they have an internal or external "tantrum" against the anguished feelings of deprivation they experience at setting these unpleasant limits. Only spenders who are "recovering" (like me!) are willing to deprive or deny themselves this instant-gratification, peak-experience "high" for the deeper pleasure of meeting longer-term goals with their money.

Money avoiders tend to be spenders (most people are a combination of types). They are often in a fog about money—either because they feel inadequate to deal with it, or because they think that money is unimportant, or because they want someone else to take care of it for them. They might well be in debt, partly from an aversion to keeping track of where the money is going, and to knowing what expenses are coming up. They might even avoid opening bills if they feel too overwhelmed at the prospect.

Money worriers are often hoarders, but spenders can be worriers, too. Worriers worry constantly (or some of them worry on and off, but intensely!) about whether they'll have enough money, whether they'll be audited after filing taxes, whether their investments are doing well enough to give them real financial security. When it comes to debt, worriers hate this, and will try to avoid it if possible. But if they are spenders as well as worriers, that'll be hard to do.

Money monks think that money is dirty, that it will corrupt them or make them compromise their values, either politically, spiritually, or both. (Many ex-hippies and some religious individuals fall into this category.) They don't like to focus on money, especially not on it growing, unless they happen to have more than enough money to give away to make the world a better place. They will either tend not to be in debt (because most of them are not spenders), or if they are in debt from avoiding noticing where their money is going, it will be hard to help them focus on their money behavior. Why? Because they see the act of focusing on money as morally flawed in itself.

Money amassers love to save, spend (on certain things—often power or status related) and especially to plan for and watch their money grow. To them, money equals power and prestige, and they will tend not to be in debt. If they are, it will bother them. They need to feel that their money is increasing to feel okay in the world. What may be imbalanced in this type is their tendency to focus on money and whether it's growing to an intense degree that may compromise their life balance when it comes to loved ones and finding enough time for other equally important parts of life—(quality time, vacation time, down time, time for hobbies and resting, and so on).

Risk-takers love the thrill of the ride when it comes to investing, gambling at the track, taking high risks with their money. They might well be in debt from the roller-coaster ride that their finances will take, and the hard work of getting out of debt might feel too unexciting and replete with drudgery to motivate them to stay with the program.

Risk-avoiders tend to be so afraid to take risks with their money for fear of losing more (or of losing everything) that if they are in debt, and if there are actions they could take to generate more money but which involve some risk, they may be unwilling to consider this option. Many women will stay out of the stock market due to fear of loss or of making a mistake. This paralysis may be the riskiest thing of all, in terms of women needing to provide for their own future.

Did you spot yourself in the descriptions? You'll likely recognize the money personality of others in your life as well—let it shed light on your current financial situation.

Counteracting Your Money Personality

The way to achieve (or move toward) "money harmony" involves "practicing the nonhabitual" or "being where you ain't" or "doing what doesn't come naturally." Many of the most worthwhile changes in life involve practicing the nonhabitual. This leads to increased self-love and self-respect, more intimacy, more flexibility, and more choice.

So how does each money type practice the nonhabitual?

Hoarders need to learn to spend money on themselves and their loved ones more as a matter of course, without having an anxiety attack or an attack of self-loathing.

Spenders need to learn to "hoard"—to delay gratification for deeper fulfillment of their longer-term goals. For them, getting out of debt and making their money start to work for them is part of practicing the nonhabitual.

Money avoiders need to take on tasks they usually avoid, one task at a time—once a week, or once a month, or once a day—it depends on what task we're talking about. Worriers need to give up worrying more of the time, but how do you get a worrier to stop worrying? Having them write down their worries once a day at least, at the hour when they tend to worry most, and give up worrying for the rest of the day, is a good way to start. They should write down not only their worries, but how they will cope if their worst-case scenario happens. Living through their fears like this helps them worry less over time and feel more confident.

Money monks need to focus on the positive aspects of money and find examples of folks who defy their prejudice—people who both enjoy their money and live out their deeper values, without being too personally greedy or ostentatious.

Money amassers need to spend some down time not focusing on amassing their money, but enjoying other aspects of their lives, which are not money-centered.

Risk-takers need to take fewer risks, and risk-avoiders need to take more. For these types, as with hoarders and spenders, they live in opposite universes, and practicing the nonhabitual will feel horribly uncomfortable at first. But if you hang in there, the rewards will be wonderful and will exceed whatever you imagined in terms of flexibility, self-respect, and even intimacy.

Understanding your own money type will give you more self-acceptance and more creativity as you design tasks of practicing the nonhabitual for yourself. If you do them, you should reward yourself, but not by taking actions that compromise your progress. In other words: Spenders you can't spend a lot of money on a reward, and hoarders, you can't hide more money under the mattress as your reward.

Finally, if you write down or speak into a tape recorder how you feel about your new actions and attitudes, you'll track your progress and your resistance, and experience the benefits more fully.

Go!

Keep the concept of doing money your way in mind as you continue reading about how to reduce your debt and increase your cash. As you read, formulate in your mind how you might accomplish it in a style that is authentic to you.

The Bottom Line

Your way of doing money isn't the only way; but it is the shortest path to a self-motivating pattern of money management.

Reader's Journal:

Knowledge Gained:

_____
_____
_____
_____
_____
_____
_____
_____
_____
_____

Steps I Will Take:

_____
_____
_____
_____
_____
_____
_____
_____
_____
_____

Monica (Philadelphia, Pennsylvania) graduated from medical school 10 years ago and continues to earn a resident's wages of $34,000 a year. While her debts are currently zero, so are her assets. You could say she has become a professional at not spending money and getting the most out of every nickel. Considering medical school fees and international moving costs (she's moved continents and financed major re-starts twice), a zero net worth is an amazing, if not impossible, feat. How could she have done this?

Actually, she thinks it was the agricultural crisis of the 1980s that did it. Monica's parents were both adept at economics, and despite informed, analytical decision-making, they became mired in debt. Their calculations were accurate, but due to high interest rates, low crop yield, and low selling price, they went broke. This has led Monica to display an interesting pattern or set of behaviors.

As a result of Monica's parents being ruined by debt, Monica was terrified of it. Her way to deal with debt was not to deal with it at all. She didn't own a credit card, and therefore did not have a credit record. To some, this may sound like an ideal approach to debt. However, it was a handicap when she went to buy a car, make a hotel reservation, or purchase a home.

Monica woke up to her damaging pattern of money behavior. She saw that in her attempt to avoid ending up like her parents, she had gone to the opposite extreme. She was operating under her parents' financial reality instead of her own. Monica was living the life of a Midwest farmer, not a Philadelphia doctor.

Chapter 2

Discovering Where You Are

The Bottom Line

If you know where you are, you aren't lost. Getting lost financially keeps you in a state of silent panic. Finding your financial self can calm the panic.

More and more women are taking responsibility for learning about and investing their money, although many of us are still what I call "money avoiders." Money avoiders are afraid to make a mistake, feeling under-confident about investing and money management and affected by old self-limiting beliefs. Only when we challenge beliefs such as "Money is too complicated for me to understand" can we be truly free to enjoy mastering money and taking charge of it in a way that facilitates our long-term goals.

You Are Here

Like a map in a museum or a subway, we each need to find the "You Are Here" dot on our personal financial road. Once we find it, we can put our finger on where we want to go and move in that direction. If you don't know where you are financially, you are lost—and being lost is stressful. Knowing the truth about your financial situation is better than not knowing, because once it is captured it can be contained. Knowing the truth keeps your imagination from making things worse than they actually are. Without exception, clients who have been afraid to look at where they really are were relieved once they did it.

Money Patterns

We are where we are because patterns in our lives have brought us here. Patterns are sets of repeated choices we make based on beliefs we hold. Those beliefs are rooted in truths we have formed from what we have seen and experienced.

Patterns grow out of what we believe. Martha Johnson, CEO of The Everywoman's Company, for example, has come to believe life gets too cluttered, and so she vowed on January 1, 2000, to throw away one bag of something she doesn't need every day. When she is traveling, she catches up by throwing a bag away for every day she was gone. If you were at her home and it was 9:30 P.M., you might hear her say, "Oh, I've got to throw out my bag before I go to bed." She will then put a pile of newspapers into a recycling bag, go outside in her garden and pull a bag full of weeds or worn-out flowers, or run to the laundry room and put clothes the family no longer wears in the bag.

Martha's pattern is an intentional effort to counteract a natural tendency toward clutter. She came to terms with it and adopted a new set of behaviors.

Not all patterns are intentional, and not all beliefs behind them are true or good for us. One way to recognize our damaging patterns is to listen to the questions we ask ourselves. In Martha's case, a pattern of reckless curiosity took her places she never imagined, with an interesting array of outcomes. She might ask herself, "Why do I always end up in a mess of some kind?" She may not realize the messes were a result of her own patterns of behaviors. Someone watching her might answer, "You end up in messes because you act before you think."

Monica might have asked, "Why do I find it so hard to enjoy the money I earn?" Someone observing her might have answered, "Because you're afraid your money won't be there tomorrow." Monica's repeated set of behaviors, or pattern, kept her sidelined from the life she really wanted. She didn't recognize it for many years. It is quite common to be blind to our patterns until someone or a situation forces us to see them. By reading this book, you are saying you are ready to adjust some, if not all, of your damaging money patterns.

What are the questions you ask yourself about money? They may help you uncover patterns of behavior that hold you back financially. Here are some possibilities.

Question	Possible Answer That Reveals a Pattern
Why do I seldom have enough?	Because you may overspend or under-plan, or maybe even underearn. Possible pattern: flying by the seat of your pants, avoiding accountability, casual view of future needs.
Why don't I open my bills?	Because you may feel paying bills is complicated or boring. Maybe you're a bit of a rebel and don't like fitting into someone else's timeline. Maybe you're afraid you won't have the money to pay them. Possible patterns: boredom with details; pride in not doing what you're told; avoiding what you are afraid of.
Why don't I pay my bills on time even when I have the money?	Because you may be afraid you won't have enough left over for yourself. Possible patterns: compensating for feelings of deprivation; choosing immediate gain over your long-term good.
Why do I spend without keeping track?	Because you may not want to grow up and behave responsibly or you may know that it will reveal excesses in areas you don't want to change. Possible pattern: irresponsibility; denial of what's real.

(continued)

Question	Possible Answer That Reveals a Pattern
Why do I spend money on clothes instead of saving for the down payment on a house I really want?	Because you may be hooked on instant gratification or you may not really believe you'll be able to buy a house. Possible pattern: instant gratification; sense of futility and hopelessness.
Why do I resist investing?	Because you may believe it's for others to do or that it is too complex for you to understand. Possible pattern: removing yourself from the action; giving up easily when you don't understand.
Why aren't I earning as much as others in my field?	Because you may have a low opinion of your work or believe others do; you may not keep up with what's going on in your industry. Possible pattern: low self-esteem; fear of what others think; apathy.
Why am I willing to flounder financially?	Because you may not know how to stop; you may prefer it to being responsible; you may like using it as an excuse for letting others take care of you. Possible patterns: out of control of your life; being cared for; living more like a kid than an adult; sense of entitlement.
Why do I think wealth, or an ample supply of money, is beyond me?	Because you may not feel deserving of money; you may believe you don't match your definition of people who have money. Possible pattern: low opinion of yourself; expectation of being left out, uninvited.

What pattern do you think is holding you back from the level of money management and earnings you desire? Listen carefully to your answer and instincts. You do know the answer. Write it down or file it in your mind, but don't let the insight go.

Money Beliefs

Beliefs are our conclusions about what we have seen, heard, and experienced. They may be accurate or not, but they are still our beliefs and we build our behaviors on them. Our money beliefs or "misbeliefs" govern our financial choices and patterns.

Sometimes our beliefs are in line with those who have influenced us, like Monica, and sometimes we take the opposite extreme and vow to never live like we did when we were children, as Nancy did.

Nancy, brilliant and creative, was raised by a tight-fisted mother who always undergave. Nancy was embarrassed by her mother's seeming selfishness. She made a private vow to be generous. As an adult, Nancy launched a pattern of excessive gift-giving. She was continually surprising friends and family with unexpected gifts, even though she couldn't afford them. Her credit card debt was out of control, jeopardizing her family's financial health. Nancy is dynamic and passionate about life, and it is easy to picture her spontaneously buying wonderful gifts for the people around her.

Life circumstances forced Nancy to realize that her belief in generosity at the expense of one's own family was wrong. She faced it and corrected it. She built a new pattern of behavior and removed a great deal of internal as well as financial chaos from her life. She has found other ways to express her joy and love to people around her.

Money Therapy

When you explore your thoughts, feelings, and reactions about money, try to let yourself go and not censor anything. Be gentle with yourself if you come out with something that shocks you. It's all part of a positive exploration and deep learning experience. And remember, everyone carries their own set of active or retired money myths.

Olivia Mellan

Our beliefs either help us or hurt us. It is important to determine what beliefs are governing you and supporting your patterns. Look over the following misbeliefs to spot those you have adopted. If you don't find beliefs that resemble yours, ask yourself what misbeliefs you hold about money. The following is a list of common money-limiting beliefs:

❖ Managing money is complicated (boring, tedious, frustrating, useless).

❖ A person needs to be good at math to be good with money.

❖ Others need my money more than I do.

❖ There will always be someone to take care of me.

❖ I'll learn what I need to know about money when I have to.

❖ I've always managed on what money I have and I always will.

❖ I can do without.

❖ I wasn't destined to have a lot of money.

❖ The rich are snobs.

❖ My friends would leave me if I earned more money than they did.

❖ Poor people know how to appreciate life more than rich people.

❖ I wouldn't know what to do with extra money if I had it.

❖ You can't have wealth and strong values at the same time.

❖ It takes a lot of money to invest.

❖ My debt is too big to do anything about it.

❖ I trust my husband to make good choices for me.

❖ Married women who insist on being in on financial decisions (like insurance and investing) don't trust their partners.

Money Voices

Many of us carry messages in our minds from our primary influencers. As children, we have difficulty withstanding the influences of our parents, teachers, or even peers, but as we mature, we can choose to listen to or ignore the messages we received. Sometimes, however, we unconsciously cling to the messages we received as children and our financial decisions are influenced by them.

For example, a client of mine named Eleanor carried a mental message that said, "Keep your cupboards full so you'll always have something to eat." It was the voice of her father. As a child, she had often been hungry and the cupboards in her home were usually empty.

Now, as an adult, Eleanor felt compelled to keep her cupboards full. In fact, she and her husband, Clint, spent a hefty $1,200 a month on groceries for the two of them. They gradually gained weight and, instead of cutting back on food, charged $2,000 on their credit card to purchase bicycles to help them exercise. They met with a financial planner for financial advice, but didn't change a thing about their behavior and said they couldn't afford to invest.

Eleanor's message will one day make her cupboards bare, because she will likely meet poverty again in later life unless she wakes up to what her money pattern is doing to sabotage her financial condition.

Are you carrying any messages that are sabotaging your financial choices?

Money Therapy

Olivia Mellan

A very useful fiction I have adopted in my Money Harmony work is to make believe that money is a person (or force, or thing) with whom we have a lifelong relationship. I suggest my clients conduct a conversation with money where money might say something like "You're holding on to me so tightly I can't breathe," or "You don't care where you spend me, just so long as you spend me fast." This dialogue is a simple and entertaining way of defining your relationship with money.

Money History

Your money history is what you saw, heard, and experienced about money in your life. Your history is your lens on the world. Whether you grew up rich, middle class, or poor, your lens sees money from that perspective.

Your money history produces your money voices, your money voices help form your money beliefs, and your money beliefs help form your financial patterns. Left unchecked, you will yield to the natural force of your influences and may fall victim to their pull. It is essential to examine what makes you do what you do financially so that you can know you are making intentional choices based on sound reasoning.

Betty's money history revealed two strong influences: her father, who lived to amass wealth and was unhappy, and her grandmother, who had little money but lived a contented life. This conflicted history caused Betty to feel ambivalent about money. She wanted it, but she didn't want it. If she earned too much money, she risked going against Grandma; if she didn't earn a lot, she was going against Dad.

As a result of her financial frustration, Betty looked hard at her history to see where her ineffective money patterns began. An independent woman and successful business owner, Betty was stunned to see how she was still holding on to old influences. Her history produced a challenging duet of opposing money voices. In turn, the money voices produced a belief that she could have nice things as long as she didn't pay much for them. This meant she could enjoy quality as long as she didn't have to feel guilty about what she paid for it.

She had a good laugh when she realized she had lived out her money belief perfectly when she bought a beautiful classic Mercedes but only paid $10,000 for it.

Betty didn't trash her pattern of looking for good quality at low prices, but she did release herself from feeling guilty if she didn't. She replaced her old pattern with a new one based on sound money management.

This is the power of your past over your financial choices today. It is worth opening up to the possibility that the situation you are in may be due to some outdated messages and beliefs you have adopted and never discarded.

Manage Your Money So That It Doesn't Manage You

If you feel that you are stuck in financial immobility, then you need to have some out-loud (yes, I mean let the walls hear you) conversations with yourself. For example, ask yourself the following questions:

What is my first recollection of money?

"I recall_____."

Who was involved in it?

"_____ was involved."

How has it affected the way I feel about money now?

"It affected me _____."

How do I feel about my money?"

"I feel _____."

Does my money control me, or do I control my money?

It is possible to pull the plug on negative messages and reconnect with life-building ones. All you have to do is do it. Change begins when we decide that what we are doing is no longer working.

Coaching Tip

If the horse is dead, get off it!
—Old Spanish proverb made popular by Karen Sheridan, Everywoman's Coach

There are many ways to develop new beliefs and patterns. Depending on what motivates you and keeps you rolling in an improved direction, you can design your own plan. Following are some ideas to capture your imagination as you prepare to adjust your patterns and beliefs.

Bring a Friend into the New Behavior

My friend Elizabeth received a letter from a credit collection agency because she had never made a payment for her graduate school student loan.

When I asked her why she hadn't paid it, she told me that she gets paralyzed with all the paperwork that goes along with submitting her payment. Fortunately, she has no other debt, but she had no savings to pay it off in spite of her great new job. She could work out a payment plan to start paying monthly now, but she couldn't bring herself to deal with the paperwork. She felt immobilized and had developed a Scarlet O'Hara style of money management. *Anything* that looked like something she didn't want to deal with could just as well wait until another day.

Coaching Tip

If you think you are poor, you are very likely poor no matter how much money you have because that's how you see yourself and that's where you put your attention. You will always find evidence to support your beliefs. How many times have you said, "I knew that was going to happen," and it did? You create what you think about, so move from a poverty mentality into a more positive one. Lottery winners often wind up in the same place they were before they got rich. Why? Because they see themselves as poor and they somehow manage to get rid of the money. Their actions are caused by their underlying belief that they don't deserve money. Or they may believe that people who have money don't have the same values they do, which keeps them stuck in their poverty mentality. They will unconsciously behave in a way that causes them to become poor again.

I offered to help her change this pattern. We discussed her schedule and agreed to meet at eight o'clock in the morning on the following Tuesday, her day off. I sat with her while she filled out the student loan payment form and submitted one payment. Then she called the credit collection agency and asked them to work out a payment plan for the rest of the loan. Per our agreement, only then could she go out and run her errands. In Elizabeth's case, all she really needed was a friend to lean on and keep her on the task she had avoided too long.

Picture Your Misbeliefs and Desired Beliefs

Put your limiting money beliefs on notice by doing something out of the ordinary. Allot an hour or less to sit with scissors, a few magazines, two sheets of paper, and your thoughts. On the first paper, apply pictures and titles you cut from the magazines that represent your old patterns, money voices, and/or beliefs. On the second paper, apply cut-outs that represent your new patterns, chosen money voices, and/or preferred beliefs. Compare the two. Place them somewhere you can see them, or take the collage of positive patterns to the copy center, reduce it to the size of your three-ring planner, and carry it with you. The very act of using a creative process like collage to visualize your patterns will interrupt the existing behavior and pave the way for your new choices. By keeping the positive image with you, you will be reinforcing your chosen path.

Acquire a Money Mentor

Everyone needs a formal or informal coach or a mentor to keep them on track generally or in a specific area of their lives. Your mentor can be a mature friend, an acquaintance who models the behavior you want, a money counselor, or a professional financial coach. Set firm boundaries around how much you will ask of them and how much of their advice you will follow. In other words, be reasonable about what you expect of them in terms of time, and let your mentor know you aren't asking to be "fixed," just accompanied. Adjusting your beliefs and patterns is your job, not theirs. A good mentor will understand this. If the first person doesn't work out, select another.

Go Online

Virtual communities are a part of many women's lives, and you may be someone who will find them helpful in sticking to the promises you make yourself about money. Check out the following Web sites:

❖ www.everywomansmoney.com

❖ www.financialmuse.com

❖ www.ivillage.com

❖ www.oxygen.com

❖ www.women.com

Read More About Money

Go to the newsstand and try out some magazines and newspapers that appeal to you. Barbara Stanny, author of *Prince Charming Isn't Coming* and *Secrets of Six-Figured Women*, recommends reading about money every day. She subscribes to the *Wall Street Journal*, a daily financial newspaper, to keep her focused. She doesn't read it all every day, but she does read a part of it every day, even if she only has time to run through the headlines. Reading about money every day is something she discovered most wealthy women do.

Money Therapy

Once we begin learning about our money, and flexing our knowledge, we will discover there is good help and support all around us. We don't have to do it alone.

Olivia Mellan

Visit a Money Counselor

The field of financial counseling is growing, and many people are being helped by counselors specially trained to help them recover and manage their financial lives. Visit Karen McCall's Web site, www.financialrecovery.com to learn more about this field and the help that's available to you.

Speak New Words

Evidence is strong that adopting a new way of speaking will change your life. In fact, in his book *Rich Dad's Guide to Investing*, author Robert Kyosaki says, "Words form thoughts, thoughts form realities, and realities become life. The primary difference between a rich person and a poor person is the words he/she uses. If you want to change a person's external reality, you need to first change that person's internal reality. That is done through first changing, improving, or updating the words he or she uses. If you want to change people's lives, first change their words. And the good news is, words are free."

Speak your new beliefs, not your sabotaging ones, and watch your money life improve.

Ask Lots of Questions

You are with people each week who know how to keep their debt under control and grow more cash. They are a live resource for you, so consider tapping their experience. Promise yourself you will ask someone a question about money at least once a week. Be prepared with a simple comment followed by a question, such as:

> I've decided to improve the way I manage my money. What have you found useful to reduce debt (increase your cash, find an advisor, organize your financial information)?

Don't forget that it is actions that bring results. You have to act upon your knowledge or nothing changes.

> What scares me about money?
>
> "I am afraid _____."
>
> What do I know about money?
>
> "I know _____."
>
> What do I wish I knew about money?
>
> "I wish I could learn _____."
>
> What changes would I like to make to my current financial situation?
>
> "I would like to _____."

We are all different in the ways we approach money—whether earning, spending, saving, or giving it away. It's up to each of us to explore our feelings about money and where those feelings come from in order to enjoy the money we have.

Take Steps on Your Own

Many people take action on their own to set new patterns and beliefs. Once they make their minds up, they are able to make the improvements they seek with amazing discipline. If this is how you're built to change, get moving—but stay open to all the help you can get.

Where You Are: On Paper

You've noted where you are in your beliefs and attitudes. Now it's time to identify where you are in your management of less debt and more cash.

I've created a simple scale to help you easily assess where you are in cash management. First, let's look at how Monica's scale might have looked just before she realized she was living out her parents' financial situation.

Monica's Situation: Pre-Reality Check

Element of Money Management	Not at All	Rarely	Sometimes	Frequently	Habitually
Earn more than spend				X	
Pay off credit card balance(s) monthly					N/A
Save each month			X		
Invest each month	X				
Pay bills on time					X
Track expenses and income			X		
Know tax implications	X				

If she had used this grid, it would have given Monica a way to measure her situation on paper. Here's how the same grid would have looked after she adjusted her pattern of saving and spending.

Monica's Situation: Six Months Later

Element of Money Management	Not at All	Rarely	Sometimes	Frequently	Habitually
Earn more than spend					X

Monica's Situation: Six Months Later (continued)

Element of Money Management	Not at All	Rarely	Sometimes	Frequently	Habitually
Pay off credit card balance(s) monthly				X	
Save each month			X		
Invest each month					401(k)
Pay bills on time					X
Track expenses and income				X	
Know tax implications		X			

As you can see, Monica was moving to the right in each category of money management. She eventually achieved her goal of living in columns four and five.

Your Situation

How does your money management system look in a similar grid? Place a mark in each square to indicate where you are right now.

Your Situation, Now: Today's Date _____

Element of Money Management	Not at All	Rarely	Sometimes	Frequently	Habitually
Earn more than spend					

Element of Money Management	Not at All	Rarely	Sometimes	Frequently	Habitually
Pay off credit card balance(s) monthly					
Save each month					
Invest each month					
Pay bills on time					
Track expenses and income					
Know tax implications					

On the preceding grid, mark the two most pressing needs you have. Is it to pay bills on time? Pay off your credit card balance? Earn more than you spend? The two that you mark will determine the action you take first.

Where You Are About What You Know

Your increasing level of knowledge about money will produce an increasing level of competence in the way you organize and manage it. I suggest you stop for a moment and assess what you know and what you want to know. Then use the assessment to help you create your own learning plan.

Look over the following continuum and place a mark in the appropriate spot on each line.

What I Know

I Know Very Little	I Know a Lot	About How to ...
_____	_____	create a budget
_____	_____	organize my own system of managing money
_____	_____	determine what I'm worth
_____	_____	invest
_____	_____	pay bills by automatic deposit
_____	_____	enroll in my company's 401(k)
_____	_____	open an IRA
_____	_____	acquire a financial advisor
_____	_____	manage my advisors and service providers
_____	_____	invest
_____	_____	create a balance sheet
_____	_____	determine my tax rate
_____	_____	check and correct my credit report
_____	_____	open a money market account
_____	_____	choose insurances
_____	_____	write a will

In this chapter, you have given thought to not only where you are but what brought you here. And now you also have determined what you know about the elements of less debt, more cash. This information will be an invaluable resource for you as you move forward, not only in this book but in your money life.

Now you know where you are. You are not lost. You can move forward with confidence.

The Bottom Line

Your money patterns have brought you to this place financially. Adjusted patterns, plus knowledge, will take you where you want to be.

Reader's Journal:

Knowledge Gained:

_____

_____

_____

_____

_____

_____

_____

_____

Steps I Will Take:

_____

_____

_____

_____

_____

_____

_____

_____

Edie (Madison, Wisconsin) is young at heart, a bit less young in body. She used to be reckless with her money, but not anymore. In the "old days," she would often spend money until the non-sufficient funds slip would come in the mail to let her know she had spent too much. When she saw something she wanted, she bought it. When she wanted to take a trip, she took it. She wasn't wealthy by any means, but worked in an office in Madison, and enjoyed life. She now admits there was a part of her that was frightened about money, not only that she would run out but that if she faced her responsibility to manage it well, her spontaneous lifestyle would suffer.

Edie was a friend of a friend and I met her one weekend when several of us were in New Mexico for the weekend. I liked her immediately. Full of life and funny, Edie knew how to stir up a good time. On Saturday night, one of the women with us received word that her husband had just had a heart attack. We were stunned as we drove her to the airport to return home. On the way back to the hotel, the conversation turned to the sobering subject of life, death, and money. Edie's typical resistance to such things was softened by the circumstances.

This conversation turned out to be a pivotal point in Edie's life. She gradually came to grips with her money life and the damage her current habits were having on her lifestyle and her future. Even more than that, Edie came to realize that her life could be even more adventurous if she got smarter about what she did with her money.

Today, Edie invests every month, and has both an emergency fund and a "fun" fund. She does the automatic deposits and withdrawals, funds her retirement plan, and is learning to do some investing online. She has a team of advisors helping her make good choices, and she is evangelistic in her effort to help other women wake up to a money-smart life.

Chapter 3

Determining Where You Want to Be

The Bottom Line

You're going to be somewhere anyway, so make it a place you want to be, with enough money to stay.

How would you live if you could? I mean it. This isn't a question for dreamers, it's a question for you. And for me. It needs to be asked with regularity, followed by action that keeps us moving in the direction of our desires.

One reason the question is often regarded as "fluffy banter with no feet," in reality, is that we're used to pitches by groups wanting us to imagine living on a South Seas island with a yacht docked 50 feet away. What I'm talking about is the simple matter of making sure that your walk-around, talk about life—the one you are living now—is under girded by choice and funded by an intentional financial design, spearheaded by you.

Coaching Tip

I find people have the misconception that financially savvy women live for money. The truth is, some of the most giving and generous women I know are wealthy. They live for relationships and chances to do good in the world. Yes, they enjoy beautiful things and often wear expensive clothes. But nice things don't mean you live for money; they mean you enjoy quality and can afford it.

The Positive Net Worth Women

This is a book about money, for goodness sake, not about life planning. I bring it up not to confuse you but to point out that it takes money to fund how you want to live, even if you want to live a simple cottage life. And certainly if you want to live a world-traveling life. Most of us land somewhere in the middle. We want enough room in our schedule and budget to support our habits of eating and playing, learning and loving.

Many women are living a "positive net worth" life. Their lives and money leverage each other and they are enjoying a sense of confidence and control over their lives. When I say "control," I simply mean they assume the authority to make choices for themselves, to choose a way of living that satisfies what matters to them. They may be married or partnered, or not. They are pleased to share their lives with people they love and they happily intertwine their dreams with them, but they know that their life is their responsibility.

So what's the profile of a woman like this? What makes her tick? The positive net worth woman has an upbeat outlook on life and understands that she can't leave her money or financial situation for someone else to worry about. She has an internal locus of control, and recognizes that what life and financial position are when she gets to retirement depends on her—not on luck.

When it comes to the positive net worth woman, she isn't afraid of taking on debt. Before taking on debt, she carefully weighs the alternatives and whether or not the reason for the debt is a good one. She asks herself questions like: "Is the purchase going to put me in a better position in the long run? Or is this purchase going to help me else-where in my life?" She also figures out if the amount of debt is some-thing she can handle or if it will leave her cash-poor. Only after she is comfortable with these questions is she willing to commit to taking on debt.

She spends money but thinks about it first. Credit cards are only for purchases that can be paid off quickly—and are used mostly to take advantage of frequent-flier miles, double warranties, and to make Internet purchases. While she doesn't often carry more than $20 in cash in her wallet, she is an avid debit card user. She views debit cards as a way to control spending. After all, if she only keeps a certain amount in her checking account each month, and only uses debit cards, she can control her spending. By controlling her checking account in this way, she's able to keep more in her savings account and automatically transfer money into her investment account each month.

This is the type of woman who is overall-savvy. Although she consid-ers her approach to money as compartmentalizing it into different seg-ments, her system works for her. She is a positive net worth woman.

Where You Are

Remember, it's important to know where you are in order to know how to get where you want to be. So let's revisit the continuum from Chapter 2, "Discovering Where You Are."

Monica's Situation: Pre-Reality Check

Element of Money Management	Not at All	Rarely	Sometimes	Frequently	Habitually
Earn more than spend			X		
Pay off credit card balance(s) monthly			N/A		
Save each month		X			

Monica's Situation: Pre-Reality Check (continued)

Element of Money Management	Not at All	Rarely	Sometimes	Frequently	Habitually
Invest each month	X				
Pay bills on time			X		
Track expenses and income			X		
Know tax implications	X				

If she had used this grid, it would have given Monica a way to measure her situation on paper. Here's how the same grid would have looked after she adjusted her pattern of saving and spending.

Monica's Situation: Six Months Later

Element of Money Management	Not at All	Rarely	Sometimes	Frequently	Habitually
Earn more than spend					X
Pay off credit card balance(s) monthly				X	
Save each month			X		
Invest each month					401(k)
Pay bills on time					X

Element of Money Management	Not at All	Rarely	Sometimes	Frequently	Habitually
Track expenses and income				X	
Know tax implications		X			

As you recall, Monica's financial patterns were evolving into a positive net worth situation. You can see from the first chart that she was better at some aspects of money than others.

In the second chart, you see that see moved steadily toward columns four and five. The closer to the right she gets, the more her money will be able to fund her life plans.

Your Place

In Chapter 2, I asked you to complete a chart similar to Monica's. If you filled it in, look at it now. If not, I invite you to complete it in this chapter. There is something powerful about seeing our situation on paper, even in a form like this.

Your Situation, Now: Today's Date _____

Element of Money Management	Not at All	Rarely	Sometimes	Frequently	Habitually
Earn more than spend					
Pay off credit card balance(s) monthly					
Save each month					
Invest each month					

Your Situation, Now: Today's Date _____ (continued)

Element of Money Management	Not at All	Rarely	Sometimes	Frequently	Habitually
Pay bills on time					
Track expenses and income					
Know tax implications					

Now I would like you to put a circle around the two qualities of money management you feel are the most pressing.

Next, please plot where on the chart you want to be in one month, three months, and one year for each of the areas you circled. Here's a sample of how Edie's chart might have looked in the early days of her revolution.

Edie's Situation

Element of Money Management	Not at All	Rarely	Sometimes	Frequently	Habitually
Earn more than spend			X——>	1 month	
Pay off credit card balance(s) monthly		X——>	1 month		
Save each month	X——————>		1 month		
Invest each month	X——————>		1 month		
Pay bills on time			X——>	1 month	

Element of Money Management	Not at All	Rarely	Sometimes	Frequently	Habitually
Track expenses and income	X——>		1 month		
Know tax implications	X——>		1 month		

This simple exercise has led you to identify where you want to be and when in your personal financial skills. You have a plan. Now you can begin completing it.

Your Immediate Plan

Now that you have charted a plan, write it down in a more measurable way:

1. In one month I will have (asked three investors about the process of investing; read one financial book; kept track of every dollar I have spent).

2. In three months I will have (enrolled in my company's retirement plan; invested for the first time in mutual funds).

3. In six months I will have (created a workable budget; interviewed several financial professionals, maybe even hired one; taken a class on taxes).

Where You Want to Be

You've shown where you want to be short-term in your financial skills, in one to twelve months. Now turn your attention from financial skills to your life.

Let's go shopping, not for clothes but for ways of living. Look up and down the aisles of this list and let the possibilities guide your imagination:

❖ Understanding the stock market because you have investments there

❖ Reading the *Wall Street Journal*. Better yet, subscribing to it in print or online

❖ Having your own portfolio

❖ Scheduling a massage twice a month

❖ Surprising your partner with something that costs over $500

❖ Shopping for the holidays year round

❖ Taking your granddaughter on her first trip to the big city

❖ Getting your favorite chair recovered with the fabric you really want

❖ Moving to the residence of your choice

❖ Flying once a year to visit your aunt in Ireland

❖ Housecleaning once a week

❖ Art classes at will

❖ Contributing to a cause you feel passionate about

❖ Going back to school

❖ Buying a laptop computer

❖ Designing your flowerbeds with the help of a landscape designer

❖ Taking your kids to Disneyland, again

❖ Collecting your favorite china

❖ Buying tickets to a concert of your favorite singer, three states away

❖ Owning season tickets to your city's pro basketball games

❖ Spending winter weekends snow-skiing

❖ Taking tennis lessons

❖ Treating friends to a catered meal in your home

❖ Starting your own business

❖ Enrolling in a yoga class

❖ Getting your car detailed monthly

❖ Framing your grandmother's tatted hankies

❖ Commissioning an artist to paint portraits of your children

❖ Shopping at the store of your choice instead of the store of your necessity

Life is not about things or money. I'm not talking materialism here. I'm talking quality of life and the ability to enjoy what thrills you and to pass it on to others. Such a life requires money to support it. It is up to you to design your money plan in such a way that it can fund the rest of your life.

What's it take to do this? Like Edie, it requires a certain click of understanding followed by a steady determination. Since you bought this book, you must have a bit of both.

What do you want your life to be? Describe a day in the life of you. What do you want it to be? Let the preceding list oil your beliefs and dreams. In whatever form you wish, express the choices you want to live out in your life in the following space or in some other form. I wouldn't ask you to do it if it wasn't important.

Coaching Tip

Women tell me all the time that they resist writing out their life plan but once they do it, they are invigorated and feel like they have a new sense of direction. As your coach, I hope you'll do yourself this favor.

What's Next

Even if you have simply read this chapter and not done the charting or imagining, you are in a different place than when you began reading it. Your awareness has been raised, which will lead to the next set of choices. Shall I indeed take the next step or not?

As you read the book, I suggest you begin gathering the following financial information together gradually as you remember or set aside a time to pull them together all at once. It's one of those personal style issues, you know. Here's what to gather:

❖ Pay stubs for the past six months

❖ Your budget, if any

❖ Last year's tax return

❖ A list of property or other assets you own

❖ Credit card information

❖ Grocery bills

❖ Credit card statements

- Utility bills
- Rent/mortgage payments
- Insurance papers
- Check register
- Bank statements for the past six months
- Savings account statements
- Retirement statements
- Receipts for other things you're spending money on, like hobbies, recreational vehicles, traveling

The Bottom Line

You can be where you want to be financially and in life. It's just a matter of a series of good choices you can easily make for yourself. Where you are is good; where you can be is even better.

Reader's Journal:

Knowledge Gained:

_____
_____
_____
_____
_____
_____
_____
_____
_____
_____

Steps I Will Take:

_____
_____
_____
_____
_____
_____
_____
_____
_____
_____

A nnie (Cincinnati, Ohio) used to work for a company that had a stock purchase plan as part of her benefits. Annually, she could invest in the company by buying some stock at a discounted price from what it was on the open market. Because she was making a decent salary, she could afford to take advantage of what she thought was a good long-term investment.

Last year, Annie decided to move back to Cincinnati where she could be near her retired parents. The company didn't have an opening for her there so she left the job, but was able to keep her credit union account. Originally, she joined the credit union because it gave her free checking and good interest on her savings account, but soon realized it was also a convenient place to hold her stock shares. Being a fairly conservative investor, Annie had no interest in playing the stock market and never had a broker. These shares were all the direct stocks she owned.

Unfortunately, Cincinnati didn't offer the job opportunities she was hoping for. After three months of job-hunting, on top of the moving expenses incurred, money was running out. She considered selling her stocks, but knew that the stock market was still strong and their value was still growing. Not only would she not be able to buy them back at the original rate, if she sold them she would end up losing almost half of their worth in taxes. Annie checked with her credit union and discovered instead that she could use them as collateral in a stock-secured loan. She knew eventually she would be working again and could quickly pay back the loan. The interest rate was going to be less than half of what it would have been to live off credit cards, which translated to a lot less additional monies to pay back.

Annie found a job shortly after she took the loan and only had to use it to cover one month's rent and expenses. With her new salary, it took her less than that to pay it back, and she was able to keep her long-term investment! As a bonus, taking the loan and paying it back had positive impact on her credit report.

By using stock as collateral to secure a loan for immediate cash, Annie made a choice to use a positive debt strategy.

Chapter 4

Understanding the Rules of the Debt Game

The Bottom Line

When you borrow money, you enter the world of debt. It has rules, players, strategies, and a scoring system. One of the best things you can do for yourself is to learn and play the debt game well.

Benjamin Franklin had a lot to say about money and debt. I'm certain he would be pleased to see his image on the $100 bill. He said:

"Pay what you owe, and you'll know what is your own."

"He that goes a-borrowing, goes a-sorrowing."

"Buy what thou has no need of, and ere long thou shalt sell thy necessities."

This is still good advice. The principles of debt in Mr. Franklin's day are still in place today, and go back centuries before him. If you have debt, you carry out those principles in one way or another. I call them the rules of the debt game.

Rules of the Debt Game

Rule #1: What you borrow, you pay back *with interest*. Once you've signed on the dotted line, you've committed yourself to repay that loan, and then some. According to Steve Rhode, creator of myvesta. com's "The History of Money and Debt," an entertaining and enlightening online exhibit, the Sumerians were the first recorded culture to develop the concept of interest, and they called it mash, the word for calves. Herds of cows were loaned for, say, a year. When the herd was returned, calves had been born and the size of the herd had increased. These calves were the interest on the loan of the original cows. As Rhodes says, "If cattle were the standard currency of the time, then loans in all comparable commodities would be expected to "give birth" as well. Why shouldn't the same be true for money?"

Rule #2: If you don't pay, you *suffer*. There are consequences when you don't repay a loan—unpleasant ones. Urgent messages arrive in the mail, creditors call you at home, and surprise visits from skilled repossessors come to take back what you bought but didn't pay for. Avoid this type of grief in your life. Repay what you borrow.

Rule #3: If you pay your loan on time with interest and you are *rewarded*. In other words, companies in the business of loaning money will think you're great and will want to loan you even more because they know chances are good you will pay them back.

Rule #4: Your performance in the game of debt earns you a *score*. Everyone has a credit score. Three primary credit agencies in the United States keep sophisticated records of each individual's credit history, including yours. The better you pay back a loan (for example, you never miss a loan payment and you always pay your loan on time each month) the better your credit score will become. An excellent credit score simplifies life in a number of ways, from simplified car loans to a better night's sleep.

Basic Strategy: Good Debt, Bad Debt

Before we get into the players in the game of debt, you should understand that there is *good* debt and *bad* debt. What's the difference? Simply put, sometimes it's a good decision to go into debt if that debt will help you gain financially or in some other way. For example, getting a mortgage loan will mean you've got a debt to repay; but over time, your home should appreciate in value and, therefore, your debt will help make you money.

Good debt is, in the simplest of terms ...

- ❖ When the item will outlast the time it takes you to pay it off.
- ❖ When the alternative to buying the item would cost you more or put undue hardship on your quality of life.
- ❖ When the interest rate is competitive.

Bad debt is, in the simplest of terms ...

- ❖ When you'll still owe money after the item is consumed or worn out.
- ❖ When you can live without it by using some self-control or creativity.
- ❖ When the interest rate is not competitive.

In analyzing whether a debt is a good one, here is a simple filter to put it through. Will the debt ...

1. Give the borrower a legally and morally sound opportunity to get out of the debt or obligation?
2. Be used for something that has a life-expectancy of three years or more instead of something that will be gone, depreciate in value, or be consumed before it is paid for?
3. Be secured by something at least as valuable as the loan itself so that the collateral can be sold to pay off the loan?
4. Be backed by someone or something that has the ability to pay off the loan if the borrower defaults.
5. Have a competitive interest rate? If the loan you're considering is outside the competitive range, it may signal a problem. If you are a person with a history of credit problems or a low credit score, expect to pay a higher interest rate (up to 5 percent higher) to

compensate lenders for taking what they consider to be a higher risk in lending to you.

When you need to borrow money to pay for something, give the loan the security test before you sign the agreement. When you do sign the agreement, make sure you have read, understood, and agreed with the terms and conditions. Don't take anyone's word for it until you do.

The Players

To understand debt, you must understand how lending organizations work. You can incur debt from any number of sources. These sources can range from large banks and credit unions to your brother who lent you $100 last payday. The vital part in all these transactions is knowing the *terms* of the loan—whether it is a mortgage, credit card charge, or whatever form your debt has taken.

Banks and Savings and Loans

Banks and Savings and Loans (S&Ls) have traditionally had two purposes:

- ❖ Collecting money from people like us who deposit it into the bank in return for earning interest
- ❖ Loaning our money out at a higher percentage rate than what they are paying us.

In other words, one way that banks make money is to use the money we place with them and sell it at a higher interest rate in the form of loans to others. In the process, the banks' customers have the advantage of managing their money by using the bank checking and savings account services.

What is the difference between a bank and an S&L? Banks generally have broader flexibility when it comes to making loans for businesses and other commercial purposes, while S&Ls traditionally stick to mortgage and consumer lending. If you're looking for a commercial, or business, loan, shop around at several of your local banks. If you're looking for a loan such as a mortgage, shop the S&Ls in your area. By doing business with the appropriate lending institution, you'll improve your chances of acquiring the loan you seek.

Banks take in money from their customers (as deposits) through checking and savings accounts, certificates of deposit (CDs), and money market accounts. Banks also have cash reserves, which are the bank's own capital. Banks can borrow from other banks if they need to in case their customers take out large amounts of money within a day or two.

Banks use this money to make personal and business loans, offer lines of credit, grant mortgages, and invest in their own portfolios of securities. A higher interest is charged the borrowers than the bank gives to the lenders (those who deposit money) and that profit goes to the bank (of course). Another way that banks make money is in the fees they charge. Over the years, banks have found more and more ways to charge fees to their customers. These fees include charges for overdrafts, returned checks, low-balance fees, mortgage and loan processing, using the ATM machines, and many more.

In addition, some banks have trust departments. Bank trust departments earn money for the bank by managing estates and trusts and by providing personal bankers for customers who have a significant amount of money on deposit at the bank.

 Coaching Tip

It is a good idea to get to know the branch manager of your bank before you need something. Then, if you need a banker, you have someone you can call who knows you.

A customer who has several accounts in the same bank may find that some of them are insured and some aren't. The FDIC has many complicated rules, but it uses an electronic deposit insurance estimator (EDIE) to sort out the insurability of bank accounts. You can find out which of your accounts are insured by going to the FDIC Web site and clicking on "Are My Deposits Insured?" All banks do not operate under the same ruling, so before depositing your money in a bank, find out if it is FDIC-insured.

Visit the American Bankers Association Web site, www.aba.com. Click on "Personal Finance" and "Frequently Asked Questions," which has hyperlinks to other bank-related sites.

Coaching Tip

Also, I suggest you think twice about buying credit insurance unless you know you are terminal. This is insurance that covers your credit card debt or your mortgage or some other payment if you die. If you need life insurance, buy it from a reputable insurance firm. Also, many banks offer Accidental Death & Dismemberment policies for very little money. In my opinion, you are better off to keep your money.

Interest and the Economy

Interest is the cost of money. Interest rates have a direct influence on your life. The Federal Reserve raises interest rates when they want you to stop borrowing money to buy things. They lower interest rates when they want you to buy more things. They control inflation by controlling the cost of money.

The reason interest rates matter is that Americans borrow money to buy many things, such as houses, cars, appliances, and other big-ticket items. If interest rates are higher, many people won't be able to afford to borrow money for a new home, so they don't buy one. This is one example.

Take time to learn about the economy and how it works. You can learn everything you need to know by carefully reading the newspaper. Articles consistently explain the relationship between interest rates and inflation, interest rates and the stock market, or interest rates and unemployment.

Credit Unions

A credit union is a not-for-profit financial institution chartered by the state or federal government and owned by its members. Credit unions may be formed by any group with a common bond, such as teachers or farmers. It is governed by a board of volunteers who are elected by their fellow members, and can be formed by any group with a common bond. Because credit unions are nonprofit organizations, they don't pay taxes on their profits the way banks do. This means they can provide low-cost financial services such as loans, checking and savings accounts, CDs, debit cards, and even credit cards. Most credit unions protect their accounts for up to $100,000 through the National Credit Union Share Insurance Fund but check with the individual credit union before you become a member.

Thanks to the Credit Union Membership Access Act, signed by President Clinton in 1998, more people are now eligible to join credit unions through associations, churches, schools, civic groups, and even members of communities. Members of these organizations are allowed to sign up immediate family members. This definition has been broadened to include spouses, children, siblings, parents, grandparents, grandchildren, stepparents, stepchildren, and step-siblings, as well as "household members," which includes people living in the same residence as a single economic unit. Over 10,000 new groups have joined credit unions since 1998.

Credit unions are a great concept. At this writing, there are nearly 13,000 credit unions in the United States. While credit unions may offer higher rates for consumers on deposits (such as CDs and savings accounts) and lower rates on loan products (such as mortgages) than traditional banks, they may not compare with the rates that online banks now offer consumers.

Credit unions started through work groups where the facilities were generally located onsite. Unlike banks, credit unions are owned by the members who elect their own board of directors and have voting rights (because they are actually stockholders). If you can't find a financial institution that will allow you to become a customer or a member due to your past financial difficulties, ask what you need to do to become financially stable in their eyes. Then work toward that goal and re-apply. Talk to one of the officers of the bank or credit union when you want to initiate this conversation. Of course, ask whether they are FDIC- or NCUSIF-insured before you go further.

Online Banks

Over the past five years, a new type of banking institution has emerged—online banks. I would be foolish to omit mention of these institutions since they are vying for your business so heavily. In fact, purely online banks will often offer the most competitive rates compared to your local bank or credit union, simply because they want to earn your business and they are willing to make less profit in order to do it.

There are many misconceptions about online banks. The fact is, they are regulated and scrutinized just as carefully as traditional brick-and-mortar banks. They also have extremely tight security built into their systems to prevent hacking or online theft. Furthermore, online banks generally offer value-added services such as online bill paying, which traditional banks may not offer.

If you are going to be in the market for a mortgage, auto, or any other type of loan, visit online banks at Web sites such as wingspanbank. com, etrade Bank, and financialmuseBank.com. Compare their offerings with your traditional local bank and decide for yourself what you think about it.

Consumer Lending Companies

In addition to banks and credit unions, there are a variety of alternatives available for borrowing money. For example, when you are purchasing a new car, your auto dealer may offer you a great low interest rate through a company such as GMAC or GE Capital.

You should also be aware that your local appliance store may suggest you open a credit card with them and pay no interest for six months. Be cautious! Often, you won't pay that interest for the first six months, but the credit card company will add those interest payments into your future payments. So you end up paying interest on the interest. Read the fine print if you are presented this type of alternative.

Rent-to-own stores are another alternative for consumers. Typically, they will offer consumers the ability to pay as little as $10 per week for an appliance such as a television, and over time, the consumer will have the right to purchase that item. The problem with this system is that the amount of time you must rent the appliance before you can purchase it often means you've significantly overpaid for that appliance. Unless you're in a real cash crunch or have extremely poor credit, I don't recommend using the rent-to-own system.

Credit Cards

Credit cards could be considered a staple among the financial tools at our disposal. Some experts consider them a requirement in today's world. Today, you can't buy a plane ticket, reserve a hotel room, or rent a car without a credit card. I suggest you view credit cards as a tool that can help you. If you're responsible and pay off your credit card bill every month, you can use that card to help you earn bonuses such as frequent-flier miles, which is a great benefit.

Credit cards are also known as the best friend of new business owners, who often don't have the track record to get a traditional bank loan.

Often, they can finance their new business by utilizing their credit cards as a lending vehicle, and spreading the payments out over time. While credit cards can be wonderful and offer us convenience, they can be a deadly part of the debt game.

Credit card lenders are really banks. The banks collect deposits from consumers and other entities, and then loan that money out. However, in the case of credit cards, they're loaning that money out to credit card customers instead of traditional bank lending customers.

A credit card provides high-interest, unsecured loans that allow the cardholder to "buy now, pay later." This is a very lucrative business for the banks that issue credit cards to consumers. They make up to 21 percent or more on the balance due if the balance is not paid off each billing period, and new purchases begin accruing interest right away.

> Joan from Colorado told me that the best advice her sister gave her when she graduated from college and went out into the real world as a grown-up was, "Never put anything on your credit card that you won't still have by the time the bill comes." Joan remembers that when she decides whether to pay cash or use her card. She put her stereo on the credit card as well as her clothes, but always pays cash for groceries, gas, and eating out. She bought her stereo on credit because she wanted to have it before she could pay for the whole thing. However, she put herself on a self-induced payment plan and always paid more than the monthly minimum until she had paid it off according to her own schedule. She keeps herself aware of her bank account when she buys clothes and either writes a check or knows that she will pay that amount when the credit card bill comes. She says it takes lots of self-talk at first but now is so used to it that she is never in debt beyond her plans.

This is known as a *revolving account* because the holder can simply roll the new balance to the next billing cycle and pay only the stated minimum amount shown on the bill. These cards may or may not have an annual fee depending on the other "goodies" like frequent-flier points, money back at the end of the year, or no annual fee.

Credit card rules can also change frequently. What may look like some junk mail may actually be a brochure that tells you the rules of the game have changed. If you don't pay attention to it, you may be in for some surprises on your bill. My credit card company changed the envelope that the bills came in and it looked to me like more offers to get a credit card. I threw them away unopened until I got a phone call asking me why I suddenly stopped paying my bill. When we discovered my problem, I agreed to pay it immediately and they cancelled the accrued interest and late charges, due to my excellent payment record. Keeping the cardholders ignorant is an advantage to the credit card issuer but they do have to disclose any changes to your original agreement. If you miss them, you're the one responsible.

Most of the major credit card companies work hard to educate consumers about credit card debt and how to make it work for you. Next time you're in the bank or browsing online, look for information about the use of credit cards by the issuing companies represented by the bank.

Coaching Tip

Keep track of the due dates of your credit cards and other bills. If the due dates aren't convenient for you, call the credit card company and ask them to change it. In my experience, they won't want to because it is inconvenient for them. Sometimes they even have to issue you a new card if you want to change the due date. I'm real clear that I want to pay my bills once a month about the 20th, so all of my bills have to come due about a week after that. I've arranged to get my bank statement before the 20th and all my bills are due after that date. It took time initially to get everything set up, but now it works great. Remember, you are the customer and you have ultimate control over your money. Don't be bullied by your creditors.

Friends and Family

An unofficial lending institution is often endearingly called the "FFAs" or friends, family, and acquaintances. There are times when some of us need to borrow from someone we know, either because it's less complicated and they are willing to do it or because for some reason we would not qualify for a loan from a bank or credit card company.

When you borrow from someone you know, treat the loan as you would an "official" loan. Put the details in writing, including the interest, if any, you are being asked to pay, how often and how much payment will be made, what to do if you cannot make a payment, and when the loan will be repaid in full. Please do not be sloppy on loans to or from family. It is an invitation to troubled relationships with those you enjoy good relationships with now.

Secured Credit Cards

If you have a credit record that banks or credit card companies find risky, you may want to obtain a secured credit card. Secured credit cards are often a first step for people with bad credit to begin to rebuild a solid credit history. Banks offering these cards will set a limit, such as $500, on the credit card. They will require the consumer who was issued the card to deposit up to $500 with the bank, as a form of collateral. The card limit will be whatever amount is left on the card.

For example, if Cindy wants to rebuild her credit, she may choose a secured credit card. Let's say she deposits $300 in an account with the credit card company. The $300 is her credit card limit. She will be able to use the card in the same way she would use an unsecured credit card, except in her case what she charges on the card will be used to pay off her charge. Many people use this method to re-establish themselves as trustworthy creditors and gradually work up to a high balance and eventually a non-secured card.

Secured Debt

Now that you've learned who the players are in the debt game, we're going to discuss types of debt. Fundamentally, there are two types of debt: secured and unsecured.

The type of debt you "play" with in the debt game may depend on a variety of factors such as your credit rating, the type of product you're trying to purchase with debt, and regulatory limitations.

When a person or institution loans us money, they want to know when they will get their money back, how much they will be paid for their faith in us that they will get it back, and what will happen if we don't pay it back. If a debt is secured by something, the lender expects that if we don't hold up our end of the agreement, they can go to the security or collateral on the agreement and collect what is owed them.

If a debt is secured, it means you, as the borrower, will only receive the loan if you can offer collateral of some type to the borrower. In essence, if the lender expects either you (based on your credit history) or the loan to be risky, the lender will request collateral, or something with a value equal to the amount you are borrowing. The lender requires this to ensure that if you don't hold up your end of the agreement, the company can collect on the loan by using the collateral to recoup what is owed.

What exactly is collateral? Collateral is something of value that we already own that can be used as a guarantee that a borrower will pay back that loan. Collateral can range from a car, boat, jewelry, or a house, depending on the size of the loan.

Similarly, if we rent a home, the landlord often takes a month's rent in advance, the final month's rent, and a security deposit at the time you sign the rental agreement. The money you give the landlord secures your lease agreement that you will, in fact, move in when you said you would, you will not leave without paying your last month's rent, and you will leave the home in the condition you found it when you moved in.

Students often cannot come up with that much money up front. They may ask their parents to co-sign on the lease, making the parents liable to the security on the rental agreement. That way, the landlord has recourse through either of the co-signers to get the money owed according to the rental agreement.

When you borrow money to buy a home, the mortgage lender will probably require you to put money toward the house as a down payment. The lender doesn't want 100% of its money in the home in case it loses value before the loan is paid. The lender holds the title of ownership for the house until you pay it off.

Coaching Tip

Not all people make money on houses. Make sure you are buying a home in a desirable location. Don't put more money into your house than you will get out of it when you sell it, unless you plan to live in it for a long time and want to enjoy it. Again, make choices consistent with your financial goals and your personal goals. They aren't always compatible. But if you know what you want, you can make an informed choice even if it isn't the best financial decision. Lenders want you to have your own money invested so you won't walk away from the house if things get tight.

Co-signing on a loan is, in a sense, a form of secured lending. Agreeing to be a co-signer on someone else's loan can be a gracious thing to do for a friend or relative, but remember that business is business. Before you agree to put your signature on the agreement, be sure that you have read the terms and conditions of the contract and know what you are about to sign for. Although the borrower assures you that her plans are good and that she has no intention of not paying back her loan, "debt happens" and you may be the one ending up paying off the loan.

One of my clients was a 55-year-old widow who had most of her savings in a 401(k) tax-deferred retirement savings plan and an IRA that had been left to her by her husband. Her son decided to go into the carpet-cleaning business and needed money to buy the franchise, a van and the cleaning equipment. He was confident that this was going to be a booming business, and he had dreams of a fleet of vans and a number of employees. He had dropped out of college and had only a few hundred dollars in savings to start his business.

His mother was pleased with his entrepreneurial spirit and agreed to co-sign his loan with the bank to start the business. Because her savings were all in tax-deferred retirement accounts, she became liable for the taxes at her current interest rate of 28 percent and a 10 percent penalty because she was not yet 59½. Even though the money was still in her savings accounts, she triggered these IRS events when she agreed to use them for collateral on her son's loan.

Unfortunately, after a year in the business, her son had developed an allergy to the cleaning chemicals and had to abandon his business. Guess who got stuck with the loan payments! Mother will now have to work much longer than she had planned.

I love my kids, but I don't think we as parents owe them as much as we often think we do in terms of financial help. We love and care for them as parents. We may help them to get started in a business or a career if we can afford to and choose to without guilt or obligation. But we are not required to jeopardize our own well-being or retirement to help our adult children financially.

 ## Coaching Tip

Think long and hard about giving your adult children money. Don't keep them from spreading their wings and learning their life lessons. This is one of the hardest things for a mother to do—let her child fall on his face. If you do loan your adult children money, do it as a formal business transaction.

Unsecured Debt

Credit cards are by far the most used, and often abused, way for us to get whatever we want right now and worry about how we are going to pay for it later. It's easy enough for us to overspend in person, when we hand over our card or write a check, but now we can do it over the phone or the Internet. It is getting easier and easier to pile up debt, which is why you and I must keep getting smarter and smarter about how we spend our money and our credit card balance.

Each time you put something on your credit card and don't pay it off at the next billing cycle, you are making a long-term debt out of a short-term purchase. The retailer or service provider is paid immediately, so they have no risk and find it easy to entice you to buy their products, even if you can't afford them.

Credit cards can often help us face emergencies or opportunities that can advance us to our goals. The point is to be in control of our credit cards, not the other way around.

Coaching Tip

If you refinance your house to pay off your credit cards, you may pay for a dinner or a vacation for thirty years. Make sure it's worth it. I have a client who keeps an extra checkbook ledger in her handbag. She writes down her credit card purchases as if they were checks. She has no surprises at the end of the month. Good idea!

Charge Cards

A charge card is another form of unsecured debt. It has no provisions for incurring debt, because it requires the cardholder to pay the balance each billing cycle. A great example of this is the American Express card. There is usually an annual fee for this type of card and it may be a negotiated fee depending on whether you are an individual, a small business, or a large corporation.

Charge card issuers may change the rules, too, so be sure you read the information they send to you. One of my friends was very upset when he learned that the charge card he had held for thirty years had suddenly become a revolving credit card, so he cancelled it. The truth was that the company had introduced a new credit card to their business and the old charge card was still the same. He just hadn't read the fine print correctly, and the charge card issuer lost a loyal customer.

Debit Card

A debit card is not a revolving credit card or a charge card, although it may look like one with a credit card logo on it. It can be used at point-of-purchase (like stores or gas stations) and often doubles as your ATM card. These are secured by your checking account and are issued by the bank that holds your money.

When you use your debit card, the money comes right out of your checking account. It can be used just like a credit card or check as long as you have the money in your account. One of my clients said that he uses it to buy groceries, which gives him the opportunity to get some additional cash back. That way he saves the $1.50 fee at the ATM machine and it takes less time than to drive to an ATM machine.

If you use a debit card, be sure you write the amount in your check ledger so that you know how much money you have in your account. Unlike a check, the amount is immediately debited electronically from your account when it is used.

Collection Agencies

If you've entered the debt game and you can't pay back your loan, you can expect a collection agency to contact you. While a great deal of progress has been made over the past few years in terms of the way in which collection agencies operate, you'll still find the whole experience unpleasant.

What does a collection agency do? Most of the time a collection agency will contact you in order to make sure you are aware that your loan payment is past due. They will request that you send payment immediately or they will turn it over to the courts. Although the lender that hired the collection agent to contact you has the right to use an agency's services, there are laws there to protect you as well. You cannot be unreasonably contacted for payment.

Although credit reporting is still a private enterprise, The Fair Credit Reporting Act (amended in 1996) granted consumers access to their files and limited the length of time that credit bureaus can report negative information. This is seven years, except for Chapter 7 bankruptcy filings, which is 10 years. It also requires them to correct misinformation and to share corrected information with every other credit bureau. Don't assume that it will be done in a timely manner, so stay aware of your credit report. Although we can't always control what goes into our credit record, we can do what we can to control what should stay on it.

Debt Strategies

In any game, including debt, there are strategies that will help you win. One of the easiest strategies to master is "no new cards." As convenient as they are, and even though they have helped most of us through some experiences we may not have gotten through without them, credit card debt should be handled with great caution.

Remember, the maximum limit on each card with your name on it is the amount that goes in your indebtedness column on your credit report. In other words, let's say you have four cards with a total maximum limit of $12,000. Creditors will look at that $12,000 as if you have indeed charged that much against them, even though you may only have a $250 balance on one of the cards.

One common marketing approach is to offer you a credit card at a low rate if you will consolidate all of your cards onto that card. People who are behind in their payments of other debts often apply for several of them.

The next time you get one of those offers in your mailbox, and I would guess it will be within a week since the average American gets twenty each year, look at it closely. If it looks at first glance like you have been pre-approved for credit of $100,000, look again. Find the words "up to" in smaller letters. At the risk of having it show up on your credit rating, I don't recommend applying for it.

Understand Your Credit Report

All games have scores. In the game of debt, the score is your credit report. You need to know what your score is and if it is accurate. Your credit report is also known as a credit file or credit history. Almost everyone has one, whether you know it or not. At one time or another, individuals or businesses have received information about you, including your name and Social Security number. They do not need to ask your permission to look at your credit report, but they do have to pay the reporting agency to do so.

Credit bureaus or credit reporting agencies are not governmental agencies, they are businesses in the private sector that collect information on you. Their customers are banks, finance companies, credit card companies, mortgage companies, merchants, landlords, and even schools—anyone who has a need to know about your reputation in the way you use money, good or bad.

When I was a little girl in Iowa and my grandma was trading her eggs for groceries, storekeepers often had accounts open for people to buy groceries and other things the general store sold. If I went to the store to get some things for my mother, Grandpa Jackson (as he was called by all the kids in town) would just write it on my parents' account and my dad would go in and pay up the account when he got paid. Everyone in the township knew everyone else and their business, so storekeepers knew who they could extend these open accounts to and who they wouldn't.

People made businesses of gathering information on people in communities, and merchants would have a database to share so they could determine the credit-worthiness of those who wanted credit extended to them. A credit application form came from that idea, and as there became more and more need to see information about someone, files were gleaned from public records such as tax liens, bankruptcies, judgments, and anything anyone reported against the individual.

Today, there are thousands of credit bureaus collecting all sorts of information on consumers. Much of it is entered manually, and the error rate is huge. In March 1999, the U.S. Public Interest Research Group reported that 70 percent of credit reports in their sample contained mistakes or errors of some kind and 29 percent contained serious errors that could be used to deny credit; 19 percent of the credit reports contained accounts that could not be identified or did not belong to the consumer; and 26 percent contained credit accounts that were closed by the consumer but listed as open. (Source: U.S.PIRG, *Mistakes Do Happen,* March, 1999 www.pirg.org/consumer/credit/mistakes/index.htm.)

Test Your Debt Savvy

Okay, let's see how you might play the debt game. Read the following situations and see what you'd recommend based on what you know about debt.

(1) You need $4,500 now. It is an emergency. What will you do? What if it isn't an emergency—how might this change your strategy?

Ideas: An emergency requires fast action. If you don't have the cash, you need to get some, and credit cards or a personal loan from an FFA would likely be the source. If it is not an emergency, sell something you own of that value or get a part-time job for a month or two.

(2) You need over $5,000 within four weeks for an important opportunity but not an emergency.

Ideas: Work a second job, sell your car for a while and take public transportation.

(3) You know you're going to be late paying a loan.

Ideas: You see where you can find the money to pay the loan immediately; you call the creditor and say you'll be late on the payment; call the creditor when you pay the bill or when you discover that you will not make the date you promised to pay.

(4) You are preparing to buy a home.

Ideas: Study the housing market in your area; ask friends about their agents and if they would recommend her to you; get to know an appraiser to find out the inside opinion on preferred areas of town; get pre-approved for a loan; shop the best mortgage companies.

We all play the debt game because there are times we must borrow to meet challenges and take advantage of opportunities. The important thing to remember is that as long as you are controlling the amount of your debt and paying it off in a timely way, you are ahead of the game.

The Bottom Line

Debt is not our enemy. Bad credit habits are. Play well and play smart.

Reader's Journal:

Knowledge Gained:

_____
_____
_____
_____
_____
_____
_____
_____
_____
_____
_____

Steps I Will Take:

_____
_____
_____
_____
_____
_____
_____
_____
_____
_____
_____

Rosemary (Phoenix, Arizona) learned the hard way about how easy it was to fool herself with credit cards. When she graduated from high school and got her first job, she didn't have any credit at all—good or bad. So she decided that if she had a credit card or two, she could establish some credit and be able to buy a car.

Rosemary figured that, with her low income, she wouldn't be able to get a credit card from a big company like VISA or MasterCard, so she applied for one at Montgomery Ward. It was so easy, and they gave her a 10 percent discount on everything she bought the day she filled out the card application. Then she decided that she could get more cards—and when a store she was shopping in was offering a discount on that day's purchases just for filling out the application for their credit cards, she applied. Rosemary only thought about how much money she was saving on all those 10 percent discounts. She had cards from Montgomery Ward, Sears, K-Mart, Target, JCPenney, and some local department stores—nine in all.

She didn't use them all and was able to pay for her purchases every month until she bought a car. Her credit was so good that the car dealer let her finance the car. She was on such a high being so independent that she bought and bought and bought with all her credit cards. Since she now had a car payment, too, Rosemary started paying only the minimum on her credit cards, which her income covered, for a while. Soon, the interest on the credit cards was starting to get out of hand—even though she cut down on using them—the balances were growing due to the finance charges tacked on each month. And store credit cards charged a high interest rate. Rosemary finally discovered that, even though she continued to pay the minimum payments, the balances were never going to stop growing until she paid more than the required minimum.

She finally stopped using her credit cards altogether and started paying cash for what she needed—often at garage sales—until she had paid off all her credit cards. Finally, she had a "plastic surgery party," in which she cut them all up, called all of the stores, and cancelled them. She asked every one of the companies to send her a notification of the cancellation and made sure that they had informed the credit bureau. If she was going to have anything on her credit report, she wanted it to be good credit—and at the rate she had been going, that might not have happened.

Rosemary never missed a car payment and is pleased that she can represent herself as a good credit risk due to being responsible with the car loan. Now Rosemary pays for everything by check or cash so that she knows exactly how much she can spend when out shopping. She and her daughter have become good "garage sale shoppers." Before they go out on a Saturday morning, they take only enough cash to stay in line with their budgets—again, buying only what they need and what they can really afford.

Chapter 5

Managing Your Credit to Less Debt

The Bottom Line

There will be times when you will want what credit can give you. Managing your debt well will keep your credit options open so it is available to you when you decide to use it.

Now you know the rules of the debt game. It's time to turn our attention to the management of credit, something that deserves your close attention. Treat it well and it will serve you, treat it badly and you will be its servant.

Debt vs. Credit

Debt is what you have borrowed and promised to pay back. There are several kinds of debt, including ...

❖ Student loans

❖ Home mortgages

❖ Medical expenses

❖ IRS debt

❖ Business debt

❖ Credit card debt

❖ Personal loans

❖ Personal credit lines

Credit is the ability to borrow money. There are times when you want to borrow money for opportunities that will make you more money and there are times when you want to borrow money for emergencies that life hands you. Either way, you want the credit door to swing open easily for you when you need it. The way you do that is to manage your credit well so that you have a credit score that makes you a reliable customer in the eyes of the lenders.

Your credit standing impacts you enormously. I have a friend whose credit score is over 700, a good score. Virtually any credit door is open to her because lenders know she is a safe bet to repay the money they loan her. I have another friend whose credit score is barely 600. She struggles to get approval for a gas card.

More and more potential employers, insurance agents, and even realtors are checking a person's credit report to measure their character and level of personal responsibility. Your job is to build a credit reputation that is attractive, not only so you can feel good about it yourself but so companies who have the power to give you the green light for a loan will feel good about you, too.

Managing Your Credit

Managing your credit means organizing and paying debt down in a way that doesn't limit your ability to move forward. In other words, managing your debt means keeping it under control so it doesn't begin to control the other aspects of your financial life.

For example, if you pay off, or at least pay down, your credit balances and loan payments on time, your financial equilibrium will stay in place. If you don't, it will throw everything else off balance. You will have chaos in one area of your money life and all others will suffer.

Living in debt is a reality for most of us. Getting out of debt is a goal many people don't believe is possible. We are a nation of consumer debt. We like to buy things today and worry about paying tomorrow. We pile up debt on credit cards, pretend we will pay it off in a big chunk, and end up paying minimums that keep us chained to a process that can turn the payment of a swimming suit into a five-year ordeal. For example, according to statistics gathered from wfn.com (Women's Financial Network), Americans who owe over $5000 are able to pay off only $1000 each year, based on a 20% Annual Percentage Rate (APR).

Managing your debt is simply borrowing smart and paying it off as soon as possible and always in accordance with the agreement you have signed with a lender.

When you sign a loan, whether for a home or a credit card, you are promising to pay it back. Since your name is on the line, you will want to take certain precautions:

1. Don't sign until you know all the details of the agreement.
2. Shop for the best credit at the lowest rates.
3. Borrow only when you know payback is unquestionably doable.
4. Be very particular about what you buy on credit.
5. Do everything possible to pay for what you want without using credit. If it is impossible, be sure the item you are buying is worth using a portion of your available credit.

Since your credit rating is an open book to lenders and others who can give you the green light or stop you in your tracks, you want it to be a good read. It is vital that you become an expert on your own credit report. No one cares as much as you do or has as much to lose if your report is blemished.

Know How Credit Is Scored

There is a big difference between the score I might give a high-board diver at the Olympics and the score the expert judges give the same diver. They know the criteria; I don't. In the same way, you may think your credit score is fine, but your criteria may not match that of the lenders.

Your credit score is called "FICO," named after the company who created it. Since you have a credit score, it's helpful to know what you're being scored on. The following scorecard is used by one of the major credit reporting agencies. For more details, visit www.fairisaac.com and click on "Understanding Your Credit Score."

Scores range from the 300s to above 900. The rating scale is based on computer analyses of millions of consumers and their credit histories. It gives lenders a way to know how likely people with your profile are to pay the money back in a timely and agreed-upon way.

You are scored on ...

❖ Past payment history: account payment information, public records information, severity of delinquencies if any, amounts of your past-due accounts, recency of past dues, number of past dues, and number of accounts paid as agreed.

❖ Amount of credit you currently owe: on accounts, number of accounts with balances, proportion of credit you've used of your available limits, and proportion of installment loans still owed.

❖ Length of time you've used credit: amount of time since accounts opened, by specific type of account, and time since the account was active.

❖ How many times you've searched for new credit: number of recently opened accounts, recent credit inquiries, time since recent account openings, time since credit inquiries, and time since re-establishment of positive credit history following past payment problems.

❖ Types of credit you have established: number of various types of accounts you have.

These categories are weighted on the basis of importance:

❖ Payment history: 35%

❖ Amount you owe creditors: 30%

❖ Length of time you've used credit: 15%

❖ Recent new credit: 10%

❖ Types of credit you've used: 10%

Know Your Own Credit Report

You can order a copy of your own credit report from any of the three largest reporting bureaus:

- ❖ Experian—1-888-397-3742; www.Experian.com
- ❖ Trans Union—1-800-888-4213; www.Transunion.com
- ❖ Equifax—1-800-997-2493; www.Equifax.com

Check your report for any errors. Up to 70 percent of credit reports contain errors, meaning you could be getting points knocked off your score for something that isn't even true.

Myvesta.org, a credit-counseling service, suggests you look for the following inaccuracies on your credit report (by the way, you can order all three credit reports by contacting this organization):

- ❖ Incorrect or incomplete name, address, or phone number
- ❖ Incorrect Social Security number or birth date
- ❖ Incorrect marital status, or a former spouse listed as your current spouse
- ❖ Bankruptcies older than 10 years or not identified by the specific chapter of the bankruptcy code
- ❖ Lawsuits of judgment older than seven years
- ❖ Paid tax liens or criminal records older than seven years, delinquent accounts older than seven years or that omit the date of the delinquency
- ❖ Credit inquiries older than two years
- ❖ Unauthorized credit (not promotional) inquiries—credit bureaus usually do not remove these at a consumer's request, but it never hurts to ask
- ❖ Commingled accounts—credit histories for someone with the same name
- ❖ Duplicate accounts—a debt is listed twice, once under the creditor and once under a collection agency
- ❖ Premarital debts of your current spouse attributed to you
- ❖ Lawsuits you were not involved in
- ❖ Incorrect account histories
- ❖ Paid tax, judgment, mechanic's or other liens listed as unpaid

❖ A missing notation when you disputed a charge on a credit card bill

❖ Closed accounts incorrectly listed as open

❖ Accounts you closed that don't indicate "closed by consumer"

Myvesta.org suggests that once you've compiled your list of inaccuracies, you complete the form that accompanies your report and send it to the address on the form. The credit bureau must respond within 30 days; contact the creditor reporting the information you dispute within five days; review and consider all relevant information you submit; remove all inaccurate and unverified information; and provide you with the results of its reinvestigation, including a new credit report, within five days of completion.

If a creditor disputes your claim that the information is incorrect, Myvesta.org recommends calling the creditor and demanding it be changed. Creditors must not report information they know is incorrect; not ignore information they know contradicts what they have on file; notify credit bureaus when you dispute information; note when accounts are "closed by the consumer"; provide credit bureaus with the month and year of the delinquency of all accounts placed for collection, charged off or similarly treated; and finish their investigation of your dispute within 30 days.

Finally, if you don't get help you can put a 100-word statement in your file explaining your dispute. Be sure to link it to a specific entry so the statement comes out when the disputed information comes up on your report. Some experts feel it is better to simply explain the dispute personally rather than try to describe it in 100 words.

Improving Your Score

If your credit report is missing data that could help establish you as a stable citizen, ask the bureau to add it. Send them documentation of accounts you have paid on time, including your house or rent payment, proof of your employment, and anything else that puts you in a good light.

There are other things you can do to improve your credit score, according to the vast amount of information available on this topic:

❖ Prove you are credit worthy by opening a department store credit card, charging something small on it monthly and paying the balance monthly.

❖ Pay your bills on time.

❖ Own at least one major credit card, even a secured one, and use it wisely, again paying off the balance as you go.

❖ Keep your debt-to-income ratio at a good level so a lender can see you have enough money each month to pay the monthly amount.

❖ Demonstrate responsible behavior by staying employed and living in the same place for a reasonable length of time. If you know you are going to move or change jobs soon and are going to apply for credit in the next twelve months, do it now.

You need to show at least one year of positive credit habits to prove your credit-worthiness to lenders, so start now.

Your credit score will be lowered if too many inquiries have been made about your credit history. Many times, these inquiries are made by companies wanting to market to you. You can erase these inquiries from your report by ...

1. Studying your report to identify companies you have not done business with.

2. Finding the addresses of each of those inquirers (listed on the Experian report).

3. Writing a letter to each inquirer asking them to remove their inquiry from your report. Some will, some won't. Your letter should simply state that you recently reviewed your credit report and noted that the company had made a credit inquiry. Remind the company that inquiries such as this cannot appear on your report without your permission, and ask that the inquiry be removed and documented.

Establishing Credit for the First Time

It is essential that you establish a credit record if you don't already have one. Not having credit can stop you from getting a car loan or home mortgage as easily as having poor credit.

I suggest you begin by applying for credit from local stores, charging a few small items, and paying the debt in full. This will establish you quickly as a responsible borrower.

You will also want to establish a good banking relationship that can be documented. Open both a savings and a checking account, even if the balance is small. Some experts suggest you show your credit-worthiness by taking out a small bank loan, say $2,000. Use the money to buy a six-month certificate of deposit. In six months, remove the money and repay the loan. Later, do it again with a slightly higher amount. This will give you an excellent rating and track record.

Managing Your Debt

How you manage your debt directly affects how successfully you will be able to manage your credit. So it is essential that you keep a close eye and pulse on your debt.

Here are some suggestions:

❖ Find out immediately what your true debt is. Many people don't really know. They pay the minimums on their loans and seldom look at the total indebtedness. This is denial. Knowing the amount of your debt may be a difficult pill to swallow, but swallow it you must if you are to climb out of debt.

❖ Pay more than your minimums. If you don't, you'll be paying for years on something you ate at a restaurant. Interest rates will keep you from making headway; you'll fall back instead of moving ahead.

❖ Pay on time or even ahead of time.

❖ Stay under the credit limits on your credit cards.

❖ Do not increase the number of your credit cards. In fact, you may want to reduce the number of cards you use. This is an advantage to you in a number of ways. You can collect air-travel miles onto one card and you will have less chance that you will misplace a card or have it stolen.

❖ Put money away in an emergency fund to help pay for things you would normally put on a card because you don't have the cash to pay for it. This would include things like an unexpected vet bill or flat tire.

Paying your debt down is definitely the goal you want to achieve, but having no debt or credit history has its own set of problems. Mainly, you don't have a track record, no proof of how you play the debt game.

Controlling Your Debt

Debt is a convenience, but I wouldn't want you to see it as a monthly requirement. Have enough debt to stay active credit-wise, but do your best to stay out of debt. Pay it down.

Credit is not the preferred way of handling problems or satisfying your enjoyment of easy and unplanned purchases.

Karen McCall, financial counselor, founder of Financial Recovery Institute, and author of *It's Your Money,* suggests that excessive debt has side benefits many people enjoy. In other words, big debt is in some way satisfying a side need they have. Karen suggests the following reasons a person may sabotage their effort to control or pay down their debt:

1. Debt can occupy our lives and eliminate choices we are afraid to make. "I can't go back to school until I pay off my credit card debt."

2. Debt can keep us from dealing with the real issues in our lives. For example, a person not comfortable in social situations may use debt as an excuse to not go out with friends or begin dating. "I can't afford to socialize" protects the person from what she fears.

3. Debt can help us prove we're not okay. If we have a deep-seated belief that we are not as good as others, debt can keep this feeling well-established.

4. Debt can create a gnawing fear that something is just about to happen. This fear becomes our only reality and everything is filtered through it, making it possible to avoid important life decisions and taking on responsibility because "everything is about to fall apart."

Paying Your Bills

How are you at paying bills? As I said in the first chapter, it is important for you to customize your financial system so that things like bill paying are easier for you to tackle. In fact, if you do well at customizing, bill paying will be fast and simple.

Eileen Buckley is an accountant who hates to pay bills. She avoids it and is often dinged extra for late payments. In an article for wfn.com, she describes how her poor bill paying habits were improved through online banking. She uses her bank's bill-paying service. On her computer, she merely enters the payee information, due date, and amount, and the bank does the rest. She also has the option of setting up recurring bills to pay monthly.

Eileen points out that there are bill-paying services as well, a personal outsource option requiring a monthly fee of under $10. If this interests you, check out paytrust.com or PayMyBills.com. CheckFree is another company offering bill-paying services. If you go this direction, don't abdicate your role as manager of your bills. You are still in charge, and mistakes can still be made.

Paying your bills on time is a discipline you must learn in order to manage your debt well. Find a way that works for you and get it done.

Waterfall Theory of Debt Reduction

There is a theory called "waterfall" that suggests a way to pay off debt quickly. Here's what you do:

1. List all of your debts.
2. Note the monthly amount due and interest rate for each.
3. Put them in order of interest rate.
4. Begin by paying extra on the bill with the highest interest rate.
5. When that bill is paid off, apply the monthly indebtedness and extra that you were paying toward the bill with the next highest interest.
6. When that bill is paid off, apply the monthly amount plus extra you were paying on the first two bills toward the bill with the third highest interest.

You will be amazed at how quickly you reduce your debt following this method.

I think Karen McCall's book *It's Your Money* is one of the best at providing you with the tools and strategies needed to help you create a solid debt-reduction plan.

Keep Learning

Why do something half-hearted, much less something that has incredible potential to make your life better? Managing your credit and debt have that potential. It is in your hands. I urge you to keep learning what you want to know to continually improve your ability and strengthen your confidence.

Read books, take classes, ask friends how they do it, go online. Whatever it takes, be a five-star manager of your credit.

The Bottom Line

Managing your credit and debt well is an important way to be your own best friend—and your future's best friend.

Reader's Journal:

Knowledge Gained:

_____

_____

_____

_____

_____

_____

_____

_____

_____

_____

Steps I Will Take:

_____

_____

_____

_____

_____

_____

_____

_____

_____

_____

Lisa (San Francisco, California) had a roommate, Rachel, who worked as an office manager for a local car dealership, the largest in the region. She was close with the sales staff and managers, the people she turned to for a new car purchase. Rachel came home with a gorgeous new car including a sports package and cool detailing. She raved about the great deal she got (probably around dealer cost).

Three months later, her roommates awoke in the middle of the night to the sound of Rachel's car alarm. Next thing they knew, Rachel was running down the street in her underwear screaming after the tow truck that pulled her car behind it. Only able to convince him to give her the belongings within the car, Rachel walked back to the house in tears while the neighbors looked on.

The next morning Lisa asked Rachel why they towed the car away. Embarrassed, Rachel admitted her monthly payments were about $550 a month for a $20,000 car! Through the help of a friend, Rachel was able to get her loan refinanced. It was a hard lesson that led Rachel to getting the help she needed.

Sad but true. Sometimes women are at a disadvantage when they buy a car—unless, of course, they do their homework and don't cave in at the last minute. Taking a friend of either sex can sometimes give you more confidence. Do your research online before you shop.

Chapter 6

Getting Help with Your Credit

The Bottom Line

When we're buried in debt, we need help to get out. The sooner the better. Good help is available.

Financial problems aren't always the result of poor money management. Sometimes situations beyond our control, such as divorce, death of a spouse, health problems, or a change in household income can lead to financial hardship. Regardless of the cause, financial worries can impact both your work and your family life.

At the time of this writing, Americans are enjoying a higher standard of living than ever before. So many things are available to us, employment is very high, and salaries provide us the opportunity to enjoy this good life. Unfortunately, as a society we are also experiencing more debt and a greater number of personal bankruptcies. Are we really living the "good life" when we constantly worry about how we are going to pay for it later?

Data released in October 2000 reports $1.485 trillion of consumer debt outstanding. Consumer credit grew at an annual rate near 11 percent in August, up from a 7½ percent pace in July. The pickup in August largely reflected faster growth in revolving credit. For more information, see federalreserve.gov.

Ernest Hemingway said, "Bankruptcy happens in two stages: gradually and then suddenly." Stay aware of how you are using your money and your credit cards. If you balance your checkbook every month and write down where you are as far as your debt payments are concerned, you can steer clear of disaster.

How to Know When You Need Help

Many times we don't see the signs of a financial crisis until it's too late. But financial crisis doesn't occur overnight. There are usually warning signs that indicate things may be getting out of control. For example, answer the following questions to get an idea of where you are in needing help with debt, if you do.

Yes/No   Do you really know how much debt you have?

Yes/No   Are you afraid to bring up the subject of money to your spouse and risk another argument?

Yes/No   Are you worried that your employer, friends, and family might find out how much financial trouble you are in?

Yes/No   Do you avoid opening the mail because you know what's in there, and you just don't want to deal with it?

Yes/No   Do you let the phone go to voice mail so you don't have to talk to creditors?

Yes/No   Are your outstanding debts affecting your self-esteem?

Yes/No   Is the pressure of your outstanding debts affecting your work?

Yes/No   Do you borrow money without caring about the interest rate?

If you answered yes to at least three of these questions, it is probably time to get some professional help. There are many sources for you to use, from one-on-one counseling to self-help books to online interactives.

Coaching Tip

Your body will tell you when you are in trouble with spending money. Listen to its clues. For example, if you feel somewhat sick when you buy a sweater you can't afford, you know you are in trouble. If you buy a CD player and fuss over whether you should have spent the money or not, pay attention. If you hide new things from your partner or spouse or change the prices or play any money games either with others or yourself, you are in trouble. It's not a mystery, just listen to your body for really good clues.

Debt Collection Protection

In order to protect yourself from abusive practices of some lending organizations, you should be aware of your rights as a borrower and be fully knowledgeable of the steps you can take to protect your rights. One act that was created with the intention of protecting your rights as a borrower is the FDCPA, The Fair Debt Collection Practices Act.

The FDCPA was enacted in 1971 and amended in 1996 to protect individuals from debt collectors. It prohibits certain methods of debt collections. This act designates how and when a debt collector can contact you. For instance, a debt collector may not contact you before 8 A.M. and not after 9 P.M. without your permission. It also allows you to write a letter to the collector telling the company to stop contacting you.

Before the enactment of the FDCPA, there was abundant evidence of the use of abusive, deceptive, and unfair debt collection practices by many debt collectors. Before this act, debt collectors used to harass, use obscene language, and even threaten violence against borrowers. Abusive debt collection practices contribute to a number of personal bankruptcies, marital instability, the loss of jobs, and invasions of individual privacy.

View the full text of the Fair Debt Collection Practices Act on the Internet at www.alliedtrustee.com/fairdebt.htm.

The following is a sample letter to creditors instructing them to cease further communications with you.

Dear Mr. Mist,

For the past three months, I have received several phone calls and letters from you concerning my overdue Rich's Department Store Account. As I have informed you, I cannot pay this bill.

Accordingly, under 15 U.S.C., section 1692c, this is my formal notice to you to cease all further communications with me except for the reasons specifically set forth in the federal law.

Very Truly Yours,

Ms. Debtor

Sample letter from Money Troubles *by Robin Leonard, Nolo Press 1997.*

Getting the Help You Need

Once you realize you need help, there are a multitude of options out there for you. These options range from the support of a friend to Chapter 7 bankruptcy. This chapter will examine all of these options and will help you determine the right course of action for your debt situation.

Debt Consolidation and Credit Counseling

If you have done everything you can to get out of debt and still feel that you can't do it alone, consider debt consolidation. Because we have so much outstanding consumer debt in the United States right now, debt consolidation has become a big business.

The main objective of a debt consolidation service is to keep you out of bankruptcy by helping you to design a plan for paying off your debts. This will include consolidating your debt and renegotiating with creditors for a better interest rate. If you wish, these organizations will contact the creditors on your behalf, set up a payment plan, and you pay a monthly amount for them to distribute to the creditors. They help to lower existing monthly debt payments, combine (consolidate) all debt payments into one monthly bank deposit amount, reduce or eliminate the interest creditors charge, and bring delinquent accounts current. This helps to eliminate late fees and over-the-limit fees, stop harassing phone calls, and improve personal credit rating. There is a fee for this depending on the amount of debt involved. You will most likely have to agree not to apply for any new credit cards while you are in the process of eliminating your debt. Debt consolidation can only be done with unsecured debt such as credit card payments, not with secured loans or mortgages.

You will want to inquire about the charge for debt consolidation services. Charges for these services vary from agency to agency and, if you are not careful, can be just another debt to add on top of your already overwhelming mountain. Although these are nonprofit organizations, they do have to make enough money to stay in business. At least 30 percent or more of their financing comes from credit card companies that would rather get their money back (even if only some of it) than have it go into a bankruptcy. The rest comes from the debtors who pay on a sliding scale for the service.

Money Therapy

Olivia Mellan

One of the warnings I need to offer about debt consolidation is that you need to be honest about your limitations and strengths. Those of you who have had a serious overspending compulsion or addiction should be very careful about consolidating debt. It may feel like such a relief that you will be tempted to run out and run up the balance once again. Unless you can really commit to and follow through on a consistent plan of debt repayment, consolidation may not be right for you.

Three organizations that offer face-to-face counselors to provide education as well as debt consolidation service are:

* **Consumer Credit Counseling Service (CCCS):** For the nearest CCCS office in your state, call the national referral line at 1-800-388-2227 or online at www.consumercounseling.org.

* **The National Foundation for Credit Counseling (NFCC):** For the Neighborhood Financial Care Center in your area or to receive Online Counseling, contact their national toll-free crisis hotline at 1-800-388-2227 or online at www.NFCC.org.

* **American Consumer Credit Counseling, Inc. (ACCC):** For the ACCC nearest you, contact them at 1-800-769-3571 or e-mail help@consumercredit.com.

A Favorite Debt-Education and Recovery Site: www.myvesta.com. They also provide help in interpreting the Fair Credit Reporting Act, dispute credit report errors, explain fair debt collection practices, and provide legal aid and mortgage referral.

It is imperative that you do your research on these debt consolidation firms before choosing a company. And you should interview several firms before choosing one. Most firms do good work, but some don't. Those who don't can worsen your situation.

A good way to determine whether a consolidation company is legitimate is to contact the Better Business Bureau and/or the Federal Trade Commission. The Federal Trade Commission can be reached at 1-877-FTC-Help or online at www.ftc.gov.

Debt Support Groups

Debt support groups come in many forms. There are informal organizations such as the multitude of online chat rooms and message boards that provide a community of people to share their insight and experiences with debt. One that we find particularly good in this area is ivillage's debt support group on www.ivillagemoneylife.com.

Another more formal debt support group is Debtors Anonymous. Debtors Anonymous is a 12-step program for those recovering from compulsive debt. It works as a fellowship of men and women who share experiences, strength, and hope with each other in order to solve their common problem and help others to recover from compulsive debting.

Is Debtors Anonymous right for you? To help you find out, answer the following questions:

1. Are your debts making your home life unhappy?
2. Does the pressure of your debts distract you from your daily work?
3. Are your debts affecting your reputation?
4. Do your debts cause you to think less of yourself?
5. Have you ever given false information in order to obtain credit?
6. Have you ever made unrealistic promises to your creditors?
7. Does the pressure of your debts make you careless of the welfare of your family?
8. Do you ever fear that your employer, family, or friends will learn the extent of your total indebtedness?

9. When faced with a difficult financial situation, does the prospect of borrowing give you an inordinate feeling of relief?

10. Does the pressure of your debts cause you to have difficulty in sleeping?

11. Has the pressure of your debts ever caused you to consider getting drunk?

12. Have you ever borrowed money without giving adequate consideration to the rate of interest you are required to pay?

13. Do you usually expect a negative response when you are subject to a credit investigation?

14. Have you ever developed a strict regimen for paying off your debts, only to break it under pressure?

15. Do you justify your debts by telling yourself that you are superior to the "other" people, and when you get your "break" you'll be out of debt overnight?

How did you score? If you answered yes to eight or more of these questions, the chances are that you have a problem with compulsive debt, or are well on your way to having one.

The only requirement for membership to Debtors Anonymous is a desire to stop incurring unsecured debt. There are no dues or fees for Debtors Anonymous membership. It is self-supporting through member contributions. Debtors Anonymous is not allied with any sect, denomination, politics, organization, or institution. The primary purpose is for its members to stay solvent and help other compulsive debtors to achieve solvency. They can be contacted at:

General Service Office
Needham, MA 02492-0009
Phone: 718-453-2743
Fax: 781-453-2745
E-mail: new@debtorsanonymous.org

Debt support groups can range from the formal, Debtors Anonymous, to the informal, discussing debt with your friends or family. The key is to find the group that best fits in with your needs and use the people there as a resource and network to help control your spending habits. These groups can also provide ideas and additional resources to help you get out of the debt you are already in. A debt support group should be the foundation of your plan in getting help with debt;

otherwise, a year or two down the line, you may find yourself in the same situation again.

Financial Counseling

Many people struggling with debt are finding help through financial counseling, a relatively new field that is attracting both mental health and financial professionals. Most financial counselors help clients not only sort through their debts and create a plan to get out of debt, but also deal with the issues that produced overspending in the first place.

Money Therapy

Olivia Mellan

Remember that it's okay to choose one or more experts, or a combination of experts and a support group like Debtors Anonymous, to help you on your journey. But it's crucial not to surrender total decision-making control to any expert. You need to keep learning alongside them (hopefully, with their help) so you can make adjustments according to how well they are serving your interests, goals, and needs.

Going the Bankruptcy Route

Filing bankruptcy is an emotional and a very complex decision that should be undertaken with very careful consideration. It should only be examined as an option after all attempts to control spending and credit use have failed; and the help of a credit counselor or debt consolidation plan has not been enough to get you back on the road to financial recovery.

Bankruptcy is a constitutional right, governed by state and federal law, to ask a court to declare a person unable to pay his or her debts. If the court grants the petition, a trustee divides the debtor's property and pays each creditor as much as the assets or the future earning ability will allow. According to GetDebtFree.com, personal bankruptcies are at an all-time high of about a million a year.

Declaring bankruptcy is an option that is not difficult to do, but bankruptcy has many consequences that will affect your ability to get credit for the rest of your life. A credit history that contains bankruptcy will make it extremely difficult, if not impossible, for you to get credit. Bankruptcy remains on your credit history for 10 years but the stigma attached to bankruptcy may last even longer.

Oftentimes, credit applications ask if you have ever filed bankruptcy, not just if you have filed bankruptcy in the last 10 years. It is paramount that you understand the consequences and look at all of your options in reducing your debt before you choose bankruptcy. While some debts will be eliminated, others, such as alimony and child support, will not be. So, besides looking at the amount of debt, you must also look at the type of debt you have in deciding whether bankruptcy is right for you.

If you are considering filing for bankruptcy, I recommend hiring a lawyer who is an expert in bankruptcy law. The attorney's fees and payment plan should be established ahead of time, and it is important that the lawyer communicates well with you. If you don't have a good emotional connection with the lawyer you interview, move on to another interview since it is necessary to find someone capable of assisting you through this difficult time. You may locate bankruptcy attorneys through county legal services that you can find in the government section of your phone book, through legal clinics sponsored by law schools, and through referral panels provided by the county bar association.

The two types of bankruptcy available to individuals are Chapter 7 bankruptcy, called straight bankruptcy, and Chapter 13 bankruptcy. Each of these types must be filed in bankruptcy court and requires a filing fee of $160. (This information is from www.ftc.gov.)

Chapter 7 Bankruptcy

Chapter 7 bankruptcy has nothing to do with the chapter in this book. It has everything to do with helping people find relief who have no steady income, few assets, and insurmountable debt.

It eliminates most debts, but also requires immediate liquidation of most assets. Co-signers to the debtor's accounts can be required by the creditor to pay off the contract. This means people who have co-signed notes or loans may be called upon to pay the debt. People who declare Chapter 7 bankruptcy cannot file for bankruptcy again for at least six years. And the bankruptcy remains on the individual's credit record for ten years. Most personal bankruptcies are filed under Chapter 7. A "straight" or Chapter 7 bankruptcy discharges, or eliminates, certain debts. Some examples of these are …

- ❖ Rent.
- ❖ Utility bills.

❖ Credit card debt.

❖ Legal and medical bills.

❖ Publication subscriptions.

❖ Court judgments, such as property or mechanic's liens.

❖ Department store bills.

❖ Loans from friends and relatives if they agree to participate.

Some things may *not* be discharged, or eliminated, through bank-ruptcy proceedings. This means you must continue to pay them. They are ...

❖ Alimony and child support.

❖ Some student loans.

❖ Some federal, state, and local taxes.

❖ Debts from fraud, larceny, and theft.

❖ Fines and penalties from violating the law including traffic tickets.

❖ Luxury goods or services purchased within 60 days of filing for bankruptcy, with a value of $1000 or more.

❖ Debts not listed on bankruptcy papers.

Exempt Property

Certain types of property are exempt from liquidation under Chapter 7 bankruptcy. State and federal laws govern what the debtor can keep. In some states, you can choose whether you want to file under state or federal exemption. Since bankruptcy laws vary from state to state, I suggest that you look at your own state's laws before making that deci-sion. You can also obtain that information from your state attorney general's office.

Under federal law, some of the examples of exemptions allowed are ...

❖ Home equity up to $15,000.

❖ Disability and unemployment benefits.

❖ Life insurance policy loan value up to $8,000.

❖ Alimony and child support.

❖ Qualified (tax-deferred) retirement benefits—ERISA.

❖ Personal property such as clothing, household goods valued up to $400 per item or $800 total.

❖ Public benefits such as Social Security and public assistance.

❖ Tools of the person's trade, such as mechanic's or carpenter's tools, books, and computers to a value of $1500.

Non-Exempt Property

This may be used to pay debts when you file bankruptcy. Some examples of nonexempt property are …

❖ Cash and bank account balances.

❖ Stocks, bonds, and other investments.

❖ Equity in a house above $15,000.

❖ Luxury items such as fur coats and jewelry.

❖ Hobby items such as coins and stamps.

❖ Family heirlooms.

❖ Second house or motor vehicle.

❖ Musical instruments, unless the person is a professional musician.

❖ Private pension plans.

Chapter 13 Bankruptcy

Chapter 13 is the Wage Earner or Regular Income Plan. This is used by people with steady incomes and less than $250,000 in unsecured debt and less than $750,000 in secured debt. The Chapter 13 bankruptcy process recognizes the debtor's assets but does not liquidate them. A debt repayment plan is designed to pay off as much of the debt as possible, usually within three to five years, under the close supervision of a bankruptcy trustee. The trustee requires that the person maintain a strict budget, and the debtor cannot obtain new credit without the trustee's approval. As in Chapter 7, co-signers to the debtor's accounts can be required to pay off the contract by the creditor. There are no time limits as to how often a person can file for a Chapter 13 bankruptcy. A Chapter 13 bankruptcy can be removed from an individual's credit record in seven years.

Emotional Bankruptcy

Besides the financial process of bankruptcy, there is also an emotional side that is often negated in the huge rush to solve the financial problem at hand. Many people who have gone through bankruptcy have to deal with not only the loss of assets but also the loss of self-worth, confidence, and self-esteem. For the bankrupt person, there is often guilt and shame that they could not manage their money.

Friends and relatives to whom money is owed are asked if they want to be part of the bankruptcy and accept a certain percentage of the money owed them. They often reply, "No, that's okay, I'd rather wait until this is all cleared up than to take less than I loaned. I'll get it someday." Then they make a mental note not to lend you money again.

People who are facing possible bankruptcy are usually so emotionally spent by that time that it affects their health (both mentally and physically), their marriage, and their ability to concentrate on the work they need to do to get out of the horrible situation.

Money Therapy

Olivia Mellan

Most women (and men, too) feel enormous shame at having to declare bankruptcy. But if unforeseen circumstances overwhelm you, there are times when it makes the most sense. The most important thing is to learn from this unfortunate event, and to plan for future unforeseen emergencies (have an emergency fund and save for it now) so that you never have to do this again.

If all other efforts to get out of debt have been exhausted and bankruptcy is the only way out, give yourself an attitude adjustment and move forward. Remember that your debt is just a number. Whether it is in the thousands or the hundred thousands, it is just a number that has to be dealt with. Life, marriages, or family ties often cannot be repaired but debt most certainly can be, and life should go on with a new and productive attitude toward money.

You always have the power to negotiate. It's your money. Make sure you come up with a payment plan that works for you, even with the IRS. You always have a choice. Make choices that take care of your financial matters and that support you as well. Don't give your power of choice away to anyone.

Resources

There are many good books and magazine articles on bankruptcy in your local library. There are also some excellent free publications to assist you in making this life-changing decision. Here are some of them:

- ❖ *Bankruptcy: Is It the Best Solution?*

  Consumer Credit Counseling, Inc.
  Education Department
  38505 Country Club Drive
  Suite 210
  Farmington Hills, MI 48331
  Phone: 248-553-5400, ext. 19

- ❖ *The Hidden Costs of Bankruptcy*

  Credit Union National Association, Inc.
  PO Box 431
  Madison, WI 53710
  Nolo Press
  Debt and Credit

- ❖ There is also a video that is free to loan from AFSA Consumer Credit Education Foundation:

  Central Orders Desk
  1919 18th Street, NW
  Washington, DC 20006
  Phone: 202-296-5544

On the Internet you will find:

- ❖ **About Bankruptcy:** www.pueblo.gas.gov/cic_text/money/other/ bankrupt.txt.
- ❖ **Knee-Deep in Debt:** www.ftc.gov/bcp/conline/pubs/credit/ kneedeep.htm.
- ❖ **National Bankruptcy Review Commission, 1997 Report:** www. nbrc.gov.
- ❖ **Online Bankruptcy Course:** www.arizona.edu/ic/law/ bankruptcy.html.

Back to School After Bankruptcy

Your ability to receive federally funded loans should not be affected by having been in bankruptcy. In fact, it might even be easier to get a Stafford loan, which is guaranteed against default by the federal government. If the loan is based on need, the federal government will subsidize it by paying interest on the loan while the student is in college and for six months after graduation. At this writing, the current rate on a Stafford loan is 6.32 percent, but the rates change every year on July 1. For updates on rates and for more information on Stafford loans, go to www.salliemae.com.

If you are a parent who has declared bankruptcy within the past seven years, check out PLUS-loan, which is a federal non-need-based loan designed to assist parents of undergraduate students. Bank loans will be much more difficult to get if you've declared bankruptcy; however, it is possible as long as you have a credit-worthy co-borrower.

Safeguards

We are all vulnerable to making unwise purchases. Catch most of us in the right mood at the right moment with the right pitch, and we can take a financial misstep. It is important, therefore, to build safeguards into our financial choices.

I have bought a number of cars over the years. I am very particular about the salesperson I deal with because it can mean not only the difference between a pleasant and unpleasant buying experience, it can also result in a cost savings or added features. So when I reach the showroom floor, I note immediately the rapport or lack of it I feel with the salesperson. If the rapport isn't there, I will ask to be helped by someone else. Otherwise, I will walk away and come back another time when I have called ahead and know that person is not working. This is a safeguard I have built into my purchasing style.

Other safeguards include ...

- ❖ Set a limit on the amount you will spend without sleeping on the decision or getting agreement from your partner or mentor. For example, you may decide that anything over $150 requires agreement from your partner.
- ❖ Avoid high-pressure situations.
- ❖ Carry only a limited amount of money and if you know you'll be particularly tempted to buy on a given day, leave your credit card or debit card at home.
- ❖ Write out a promise to yourself to withstand instant gratification and place it in your wallet. Or, purchase a ring to symbolize your vow to yourself of financial responsibility. Look at that ring when you are tempted to go against that vow.

❖ Reduce the amount of time you spend browsing in stores and malls.

❖ Have a spending plan and stick to it. People who do this know that not buying something you really want feels good once you walk away. If it doesn't feel good and you keep thinking about it, create a plan to buy it without going into debt.

You will make much better financial decisions if you don't care what people think about you and what you buy. For example, you can drive an old car that is well-cared-for and feel great knowing you are taking good care of yourself at the same time. No need for apologies or explanation, just live out your plan.

The Bottom Line

Do what you have to do to get the help you need, and be sure the help matches the true extent of your situation. Not more, not less. Stand tall and be full-faced in your quest for financial help and success.

Reader's Journal:

Knowledge Gained:

_____

_____

_____

_____

_____

_____

_____

_____

_____

_____

Steps I Will Take:

_____

_____

_____

_____

_____

_____

_____

_____

_____

_____

Jennifer (Orlando, Florida) is the epitome of a woman who manages her assets well. She learned it from her mother. When she was born, Jennifer already had a college fund. When she was three, she was making deposits into her savings account. Her mother talked openly about money and enthusiastically educated her daughters about wise money management. Jennifer recalls her mother taking her daughters to the bank to watch her do business with her banker. Then they would go to the ice cream parlor to talk about it. As the girls grew, their mother introduced them to investing, real estate, and financial planning.

Jennifer's mother also taught her to value her personal assets and find ways to make money using them. Jennifer has natural talent with animals, and she earned money taking care of other people's pets. This eventually led to employment at a pet store and then to a college degree in animal husbandry.

Shopping was always done carefully. She planned what she would buy ahead of time and often shopped sales and consignment shops, not because she couldn't afford to buy full-price but because she wanted to apply as much money as possible to other things, including her investments.

Jennifer was receptive to her mother's instruction and example. At 21, she owned her own home and had an impressive portfolio. Today, Jennifer credits her mother with inspiring her to achieve personally and financially. Money wasn't difficult or boring; instead, it was a ticket to an exuberant, intentional life that Jennifer still relishes today.

Chapter 7

Managing Your Assets to More Cash

The Bottom Line

Managing your assets will not only increase your net worth, it will strengthen your personal worth.

The woman who manages her assets well has an edge. She knows what she's worth, she knows how to make the most of it, and she is in constant development. She also guards her assets like a pit bull, making sure debt and poor credit stay out of the picture. She understands that it is less difficult to take what you have and enhance it than to reconstruct something that has been damaged.

Whether or not you fit this description yet, you can become this kind of woman. Instead of letting Jennifer's story defeat you, let it inspire you.

The positive net worth woman is intentional and proactive:

- ❖ She knows her assets.
- ❖ She plans.
- ❖ She seeks advice.
- ❖ She is insured.
- ❖ She budgets.

Let's look at each of these qualities and learn from her.

She Knows Her Assets

As you know, an asset in the broadest sense is something of value. In the narrower sense, it is money or something that if you were to sell it would result in money. Common assets are homes, cars, boats, jewelry, gold, stocks, bonds, trusts, certain collectibles, and notes on loans.

Asset management is simply organizing and overseeing your assets in much the same way as you organize your home, family, and career. I want to remind you, by the way, that you are your biggest asset. You are the one whose mind and actions can produce more cash through smart asset management.

List your assets and their value, if you haven't done so already. What do you have that could create more cash if you were to sell it? Complete this grid or use one of your own if you have financial tools already.

Your Assets on Today's Date: _____

Item	Value When Purchased	Value Now
_____	_____	_____
_____	_____	_____
_____	_____	_____
_____	_____	_____
_____	_____	_____
_____	_____	_____
_____	_____	_____

Item	Value When Purchased	Value Now

Now total up the current value of your assets. This is your total assets.

She Plans

Planning for what you want your life to be and for what life might bring you in the way of opportunity and challenge is essential to competent asset management. It is also the path to living confidently. When you know you have a plan, you know you are prepared. This enables you to focus on what's in front of you rather than worry about what's going to happen. Making plans puts you on a purposeful path and increases your chance to live like you want. Perhaps you are a natural planner. This is a piece of cake for you because you know how to make things happen. You can probably list on demand the things you would like to do in your life. Others of us aren't quite as adept at planning. We may not believe things are possible, or we are great at focusing on the moment instead of the future.

Either way, projecting what you want your life to hold now and in retirement is important. Write it down on paper or your computer so you'll have something to construct into a more detailed plan. Your list will be a work in progress as you discover more things to put on it.

The savvy asset manager makes plans for her retirement, for her dreams, for her kids' education, and for her estate.

For Retirement

When do you want to stop working for income and start living off the money you have saved and invested? Have you envisioned what your days will be like? It's time to start thinking that way, even if you're on the younger side. You want to be sure you have enough money to cover your wishes for the rest of your life. You don't want to arrive at retirement and find out you can't do what you hoped to do.

Mark the things on the following list that match your plans. Add to it with other things in your mind:

I want to ...

- ❖ Stay in my own home as long as possible.
- ❖ Drive a newer car.
- ❖ Be well-insured.
- ❖ Take classes at will.
- ❖ Travel on short trips and occasional big trips.
- ❖ Invest monthly.
- ❖ Save monthly.
- ❖ Understand and pay my taxes.
- ❖ Contribute to causes I care about.
- ❖ Hire advisors like a financial planner, accountant, and attorney.
- ❖ Subscribe to a few magazines, cable television, and an Internet service.
- ❖ Eat out regularly.
- ❖ Get massages.
- ❖ Get good medical help.
- ❖ Buy vitamins and prescriptions.

What will this cost you? Project and add up those costs to get an idea of what you will need annually to fund the life you want to live. Add a cushion to allow for increased prices. Your financial professional can help you figure this or you can get detailed information from the Internet at any retirement planning site.

Estimating how much you will need for retirement is imperative. There are many tools to help you do this. If you don't estimate what you'll need, you can't know if you're investing enough to make it happen.

According to U.S. Department of Labor information, if you put $1,000 at the beginning of each year into an IRA from age 20 to age 30 (11 years) and then never put in another dime, and the account earns 7 percent annually, you'll have $168,514 in the account at age 65. If someone else begins putting in the same amount annually at age 30 for 35 years straight (3 times what the first person invested), she would have only $147,913. This is what compounding does for you!

You will need about 70 to 90 percent of what you earn now for retirement, depending on where you will be living and what kind of lifestyle you choose. You will want to calculate inflation into that figure. Inflation rates vary from year to year. Estimate high. A financial professional can help you do that.

As a woman, you can expect to live longer than men, and 90 percent of all women will be in charge of their finances at some point in their lives, many after their spouses die. If you retire at age 65, you can expect to live about 17 additional years. Seventeen years is a significant length of time, and you will want to enjoy it. Enjoying these years will require money. It's your job to make certain you have it.

As you plan retirement, take Social Security into consideration. It will supplement your other retirement income.

For Social Security

In the past 12 months, the Social Security Administration has mailed nearly 133 million Social Security Statements to workers age 25 or older who are not already receiving Social Security benefits on their own earnings records. And the second of the annual mailings is under way.

If you haven't received your Statement, it could mean ...

- ❖ You've never paid into Social Security.
- ❖ You're already receiving benefits.
- ❖ They couldn't obtain your current address.

They don't keep your address on file unless you're receiving benefits. Instead, they get addresses from the Internal Revenue Service each year. Therefore, if you've moved and not reported your new address to the IRS or the U.S. Postal Service, you won't get a Statement unless you ask for one.

The Social Security Statement is intended to help you plan your financial future. Social Security is more than retirement. It gives estimates of monthly Social Security disability and survivors' benefits that you and your family may be eligible to receive now and in the future. The Statement also helps you see whether your earnings, or self-employment income, are posted correctly.

Carefully review the earnings on your Statement year by year. That's very important because your future benefit amounts will be based on the record of your lifetime earnings. An error in your earnings, even for one year, can result in a benefit payment that is lower than you or your family should receive.

If you didn't receive a Social Security Statement, you can visit www.ssa.gov/mystatement to send an online request for a Statement. Or you can call 1-800-772-1213 to get a paper application form (SSA-7004). Either way, about four to six weeks after you submit the form (showing your total earnings for last year and your estimated future earnings), you'll receive your Statement in the mail.

Be sure to read it carefully—besides helping you plan your financial future, you'll learn some interesting things about Social Security.

For Retirement Income Sources

Your retirement income will probably come from a number of sources: your retirement plan at work, your investments, savings, Social Security, IRAs, and annuities.

Freeing up money to save for your retirement is a good idea if you find you don't have enough to invest. Chart your spending, add up your bills, subtract it from all monies you earn, and see the difference. If you are spending more than you are earning, you will want to put yourself on a plan to reduce what you spend. I cover this in other parts of the book. If you earn more than you spend, you have money to put away and could put away even more if you, too, lowered the amount you spend each month. Spending less than you earn seems so simple, but so few people do it.

As I have said in other places in the book, be sure you are investing the maximum amount allowable in your company's retirement plan. This is even more important if your company matches your contribution.

If you don't work or have access to a company-sponsored retirement plan, you can either get a job that offers one or start your own. You can open an IRA, buy an annuity, invest in mutual funds and/or stocks, and build your personal savings.

If you haven't been contributing to your retirement plan, you must begin now. Get a copy of your most recent retirement contributions. Go over them carefully and make sure that everything you have contributed is in your account and that if there is a company match stated in your benefits book, it is all in your account as well.

When you leave the company, don't touch that money! You will have some choices. Your former employer may allow you to keep the money in their plan and your new company may allow you to bring it with you. You need to know which company has the best plan for you. Another option is to have it rolled over into your own traditional IRA. Before you make a decision, you might want to discuss this with a financial planner to help you determine what is best for you. At any rate, don't have the money transferred directly to you. If you are not sure, leave it where it is until you have carefully thought through your decision.

If you take your retirement money before you are 59½, you must pay the tax on the entire amount plus a ten percent penalty for taking it out too early. There are some exceptions to this and you should contact a financial planner, an accountant, or the IRS directly to see what the latest legislation allows and whether or not you are eligible. If you are 59½ or older, you will still be responsible for the tax on the amount you withdraw but there would not be a ten percent penalty.

You may hear that you can have the money for 60 days and then put an equal amount into a new retirement account. If you do this, your old company will deduct 20 percent to give to the Internal Revenue Service and you will have to claim it back on your next tax return. It isn't worth all that paperwork unless you absolutely need to give yourself a 60-day loan and you know for sure where the money will come from before the 60 days is up. There are much better ways to give yourself a loan.

For Your Dreams

Life is for many things; one of them is to live out your dreams. I've addressed this before, but I ask it again: What are your dreams? How do you want to live now and in retirement? What do you want said about you after you're gone? Live your legacy.

Force yourself to make these choices. Keep them flexible, but flex your mind around the topic. It's your life, after all. No one else should make these decisions for you.

My friend Maureen and her husband, Jake, bought a fifth wheeler and travel the country since they retired early. This was Jake's dream, not hers. She wasn't opposed to it, it just wasn't what she thought she would be doing. At first she resented it, then she realized she had never done what her husband did: figure out what mattered to her in retirement. Fortunately for both of them, Janice learned to love traveling, but she also added her own piece to the picture. She always wanted to be a landscape photographer. She took classes, bought a camera and the goodies that go with it, and now takes beautiful pictures around the United States. She is even placing them on a Web site she designed for herself.

For Her Children's Education

You could do what Jennifer's mother did. You could fund your children's education even before they are born. If you already have kids, there are a number of education plans you can invest in to be sure your children can attend the college of their choice. This is true of grandchildren as well.

Some women beat themselves up if they don't have enough money to give their kids a full tuition ride to college. Don't do that. Pay what you can and help them figure out the rest. Kids do it all the time.

For Her Estate

My friend Susan says she's going to do her best to spend all of her money before she dies so she can enjoy every dollar she earned. She loves her kids but figures they can work out their own money life without her giving them a bundle.

Her sister Grace, on the other hand, has gone to great lengths to put money away for the children to inherit.

These women came to their decisions based on their own values. You need to do the same.

Once you determine what you want to leave to those people and causes you love, contact a financial professional to help you craft your plan.

She Seeks Advice

As a certified financial planner, people tell me that they wish they were "wealthy enough to need a financial planner." They think I'm kidding when I tell them that most of my clients have become wealthy *because* they have a financial planner.

Choosing a financial planner carefully is as important as choosing a family physician. You need someone to help guide you to financial well-being. Finding someone who listens to you and communicates with you at your level of understanding is more important than having someone who has half the alphabet on his or her business card. You can only find the right person with face-to-face interviews.

Money Therapy

Olivia Mellan

Financial seminars, workshops, and clinics can be a good way to help you understand the language of finance and translate it to your own situation. Attend an Everywoman's Money Conference in your area or any one of their follow-up classes. Every town has its own classes offered by local professionals. It's a great place to scout out advisors.

Anyone can be called a "financial planner." They can hang out their shingle and begin accepting clients. As long as they don't have more than fifteen clients, they don't even have be a Registered Investment Advisor, which is merely a registration and takes no amount of education to attain; no regulatory agency monitors their activities. According to the College for Financial Planning in Denver, Colorado, "Financial planning is the process in which coordinated, comprehensive strategies are developed and implemented for the achievement of financial goals."

You may be considering help from a financial planner for a number of reasons, whether it's helping you to get out of debt, deciding to buy a new home, planning for retirement or education, or simply not having the time or expertise to get your finances in order. Whatever your needs, working with a financial planner can be a helpful step in securing your financial future.

In your search for a financial planner, start with the professionals. To find a financial planner in your area contact any of these professional organizations:

Financial Planning Association
1-800-282-PLAN (1-800-282-7526)

National Association of Personal Financial Advisers
1-888-FEE-ONLY (1-888-333-6659)

Certified Financial Planner Board of Standards
1-888-CFP-MARK (1-888-237-6275)

You will want to select a competent, qualified professional with whom you feel comfortable, one whose business style suits your financial planning needs. It will give you what to look for when interviewing financial planners and asking these questions:

1. What experience do you have?
2. What are your qualifications?
3. What services do you offer?
4. What is your approach to financial planning?
5. Will you be the only person working with me?
6. How will I pay for your services?
7. How much do you typically charge?
8. Could anyone besides me benefit from your recommendations?
9. Have you ever been publicly disciplined for any unlawful or unethical actions in your professional career?
10. Ask the planner to provide you with a written agreement that details the services that will be provided.

Keep this document in your files for future reference. (Source: Certified Financial Planning Board of Standards)

Coaching Tip

Stockbrokers are paid by commissions and they should not be your overall financial planning advisor. Neither should attorneys. Estate planning attorneys have knowledge of how estate taxes affect financial planning, but unless there is no other financial advising service where you live, attorneys should be paid for practicing law, not for filling out your tax returns.

Certified Financial Planner (CFP) Board

The Certified Financial Planner (CFP) Board Web site (www. CFP-Board.org) is an online resource for information about CFP licensees and the financial planning profession. The CFP Board is a nonprofit professional regulatory organization founded in 1985 to benefit the public by fostering professional standards in personal financial planning.

Individuals who meet rigorous certification requirements are licensed by the CFP Board to use its trademarks CFP and Certified Financial Planner. A certified financial planner who can use the CFP designation must graduate from a CFP Board–approved college, have at least three years of financial planning experience, pass a rigorous exam, and have no criminal or major regulatory record.

Consumers can call the CFP Board to confirm whether a financial planner is currently licensed to use the CFP trademarks, to determine if a CFP licensee has ever been publicly disciplined, or to lodge a complaint against a CFP practitioner.

> Certified Financial Planner
> Board of Standards (CFP Board)
> 1700 Broadway, Suite 2100
> Denver, CO 80290-2101
> Phone: 303-830-7500
> Toll-free: 1-888-CFP-MARK (1-888-237-6275)
> Fax: 303-860-7388
> E-mail: mail@CFP-Board.org
> Web site: www.cfp-board.org

The Certified Financial Planner Board of Standards Web site has a brochure that you can download, *Ten Questions to Ask When Choosing a Financial Planner*. (If you need to, you can request it be sent by mail.)

The questions in this brochure will help you interview and evaluate several financial planners to find the one that's right for you.

National Association of Insurance Commissioners (NAIC)

Contact NAIC to be directed to your state agency that regulates insurance. Then check to see if the financial planer is licensed to sell insurance or has any insurance violations.

> National Association of Insurance Commissioners (NAIC)
> 120 W 12th Street, Suite 1100
> Kansas City, MO 64105
> Phone: 1-816-842-3600
> Web site: www.naic.org

National Association of Securities Dealers (NASD)

The NASD is an association of the firms that sell securities and are referred to as a *self-regulatory organization*, an SRO. That means they police their own members (sort of like hiring the fox to guard the hen house). If your advisor sells products, then check them out here.

You can also check with the NASD to obtain the disciplinary history of registered representatives and broker/dealers. This is kept in a central registration depository (CRD file).

> National Association of Securities Dealers (NASD)
> 1735 K Street, NW
> Washington, DC 20006
> Phone: 1-800-289-9999
> Web site: www.nasdr.com

National Fraud Exchange (NAFEX)

NAFEX offers consumers the ability to run background checks on financial planners, real estate agents, brokers, trust advisors, and mortgage officers for a fee of $39 for the first individual and $20 per person for further background checks. The background checks reveal if the person has been the subject of a criminal, civil, enforcement, or administrative action in the securities or financial services industry.

> National Fraud Exchange (NAFEX)
> 12020 Sunrise Valley Drive, Suite 360
> Reston, VA 20191
> Phone: 1-800-822-0416

North American Securities Administration Association (NASAA)

NASAA is an organization of state securities administrators. Consumers can check with NASAA to find out which state agency regulates the state securities-licensed financial planners. These are planners with less than $25 million under management. Each state has a different agency regulating planners; call and find out who guards the hen house in your state. The NASAA also provides a free pamphlet, *How to Check Out a Broker*.

> North American Securities Administration Association (NASAA)
> One Massachusetts Avenue, Suite 310
> Washington, DC 20001
> Phone: 202-737-0900
> Web site: www.nasaa.org

Securities and Exchange Commission (SEC)

The SEC is a federal agency that governs the securities industry. They are one of the "good guys" in Washington because they look out for the investor. If your planner calls themself an RIA (Registered

Investment Advisor) and has more than $25 million under management, they should be registered with the SEC.

Securities and Exchange Commission (SEC)
450 5th Street, NW
Washington, DC 20549
Phone: 1-800-732-0330
Web site: www.sec.gov

Accountants

Choosing the right accountant follows the same guidelines as choosing any other financial advisor. While your accountant is the person you hire to dot the i's and cross the t's on your tax return, personal communication is extremely important. You are responsible for keeping your information together all year, but there will be times when you have questions and you want someone who will listen to you and be able to answer your questions in clear form without endangering your self-esteem.

If your accountant asks if you understand, don't nod your head if you really don't understand. As my mother said, no decision has to last forever and that includes working with advisors with whom you are not comfortable.

Finding a proactive accountant, one who goes beyond just preparing your tax returns, can help you to be in control of your money. While tax compliance involves filling out the correct forms and being sure that you get them in on time, knowing the tax laws with all of the changes and helping you to structure your finances to minimize taxes is what you pay your accountant for. Tax planning is long-range planning. Your accountant can help you to deal with the tax ramifications of everything from buying or leasing a car to buying a home, retirement planning, getting a divorce, and settling an estate.

Many financial professionals can assist you with taxes, including simple tax preparers, financial planners, attorneys, and even some insurance agents. But a certified public accountant (CPA) is the only financial professional licensed to do so. Like certified financial planners, CPAs have taken a rigorous two-day exam and must comply with continuing education requirements and renew their licenses, so the advice they give you should always be current.

If you have your own business, you should use the same CPA for both the business and your personal taxes because the two dovetail in your overall tax planning.

Big accounting firms may have wonderful credentials with specialized accountants, but I recommend working with a small firm where you will be able to develop a lasting relationship with the same person.

You can find a CPA in your local area by contacting the American Institute of Certified Public Accountants, Personal Financial Planning Division at 1-800-862-4272.

She Is Insured

Insurance agents can often perform some financial planning work with their clients. An insurance agent with a ChFC designation has taken courses and passed an exam to advise their clients in financial planning. Remember, though, that while insurance agents often offer "free" financial planning, they get paid from the commissions from the products they sell.

You can find these licensed advisors by contacting the American Society of CLU & ChFC at 1-800-392-6900.

Although insurance agents are helpful in deciding what kinds of insurance we need and how much, remember that those agents are paid by commission on the amount of dollars their clients are willing to pay for premiums. You must be the one in control of those decisions and use the insurance agent to help you to find the best insurance to meet your goals. Don't buy more insurance than you need.

To understand how insurance works, imagine that you are saying to the insurance provider, "I'll bet I have a loss (of income, property, health, ability to work). So I will pay a little every year and expect you to pay the large amount when my loss occurs." And the insurance company says to you, "We'll take that risk and bet that you won't have a loss but we'll collect money from all of our policyholders so that it will be there for those who win this bet."

Buying appropriate insurance is our opportunity to keep ourselves from going into debt because we have an unforeseen loss, which would cost us more money than we have to recover the loss.

Disability Insurance

Disability insurance is the most underutilized insurance vehicle available to us. It can replace a portion of our income when we have to leave the workforce because of injury, chronic illness, or other disability that keeps us from earning an income. Most disability insurance companies will insure between 60 percent to 70 percent of your income, but that can vary with the policy.

Most people feel that if they become disabled, either temporarily or permanently, their employer's disability insurance will cover them. This may or may not be true, so check your policy carefully. But what if you lose your job or are self-employed?

Disability insurance policies vary from one employer to another and from one insurance company to another. Short-term policies may provide up to two years of coverage, although they are usually shorter—more like 13 to 26 weeks. They may also pay you more money than long-term policies, which might last until you are 65 and can qualify for Medicare, the federal health insurance program for older Americans.

Disability is determined by two standards: "own occupation" and "any occupation." The "own occupation" policy is usually more expensive because it insures you if you cannot continue in the job you were doing before you became disabled. "Any occupation" means that you are unable to perform any kind of gainful employment.

More people between the ages of 35 and 65 become disabled than die. One in eight of us face possible disability sometime in our lives. It is important to know the terms of disability insurance you have through your work, or you need to get your own policy if you don't have disability insurance through your job. Social Security Disability Insurance (SSDI) has a very broad definition of disability; at this time about 70 percent of people who apply for this public disability insurance are denied.

If you have a pre-existing condition, you may not be able to buy private disability or life insurance. If you are the sole source of income for your family, you need to find money in your budget to cover the costs of these policies.

If you are positive that you will always be employed by the same company (something few of us can say), you may be able to save those premium costs by not having a private disability policy. But if your family is dependant on your employment wages, and you are not sure of your job security, disability insurance should be seriously considered. If you have had a disabling illness, you may not be eligible to purchase a disability policy due to your "pre-existing condition." Employers usually have a broad definition of "pre-existing condition," if any at all. Just be sure that you know your company's benefits and check this out with a new employer before you accept a new position with them.

When you are shopping for a disability insurance policy, you need to consider the waiting period before you receive benefits. The longer the waiting period, which might be anywhere from 30 to 180 days, the lower the premium. If the waiting period is 180 days, and you and your family are depending on your income, you will need to keep your emergency reserve at six months of expenses. You should also be sure that your policy has a *waiver of premium,* which eliminates your need to pay the premium while you are disabled.

Life Insurance

Life insurance should be considered if someone is depending on you to take care of them financially. If you have no dependents and you will leave enough money at your death to pay for your debts and funeral and burial expenses, you might not need any life insurance.

There are basically two types of life insurance: term insurance and permanent insurance. If you have a temporary insurance need such as having young children who will eventually support themselves, or you are supporting aging parents whom you are likely to outlive, term insurance would probably be your best choice. The premiums are lower than those for permanent insurance, and the younger you are, the lower the premiums. Policies remain in effect for a specified period of time such as 5, 10, or 15 years—as long as you pay the premiums, which may stay constant during that period and then increase at the renewal period. It would also be wise to get a policy that is guaranteed renewable in case your health should change.

You might think of term insurance as renewing every year; when the premiums are no longer paid (after a specified grace period) the policy is terminated. Term insurance pays the face value at the time the insured dies, but it has no cash value so you cannot borrow against it.

Common permanent life insurance policies are whole life, universal life, and variable life. These differ from term insurance in that, while they pay the death benefit at the death of the insured, they may have some cash value, which you can borrow against at an interest that is usually lower than your credit cards. If you die before you pay back the amount of the loan, that amount is deducted from the death benefit. While permanent insurance premiums are higher than term insurance premiums, some of the premium is used to pay for the death benefit and some of it provides for the savings or investment cash value. If you can be a diligent saver or investor, you may want to "buy term and invest the rest" if you have a temporary life insurance need.

Insuring Your Home and Auto

Another insurance need many of us must have is homeowner's insurance, and if we own rental property we will need landlord's insurance. If we value our personal belongings and are not able to replace them with our own funds, we may need renter's insurance. Many landlords require this of their tenants. This is not very expensive insurance, but shop around for the best price for the coverage you will receive.

Auto insurance is required by most states, and rates vary by state according to the type and age of the vehicle, the age of the insured, and the amount of coverage. If your car is an old one, you may decide to lower your premium and drop the collision part of your coverage. If you do have damage to your car, you may need to use some of your emergency reserve to repair it.

Medical Insurance

With rising healthcare costs, no one in the United States should be without medical insurance coverage. If you can't get medical insurance for you or your children, look into a Medical Savings Account, which allows you to put aside pre-tax money to cover healthcare. The best way to get health insurance is through an employer, but a good health insurance broker can help find suitable insurance to fit your budget. Information related to this can be difficult to find for those unable to afford health insurance.

Long-Term-Care Insurance

We women are more than twice as likely as men to enter a nursing home after we turn 65. In fact, we make up 75 percent of the nursing home population. The cost of this can easily run $60,000 a year, compared to home care, which is about $40,000 a year. The average stay in a nursing home is one to three years. By the time today's 55-year-olds hit 76 years of age, the cost of nursing home care is predicted to be between $120,000 and $150,000 a year. This is just to live there, and does not include medications or special services. Here's one more reason to invest in yourself and in your health.

The costs of long-term-care policies increase incrementally with age. Work with an insurance agent who represents several long-term-care companies to design the plan that best fits you and what you can afford. Be sure that you understand the choices you have from the whole array of plans before you sign a contract.

Insurance Synopsis

The following is a list of things you should remember about insurance:

- ❖ Insurance is the way you can cover the expense of losses that are larger than you can afford, as long as you pay the premiums.
- ❖ Buy insurance to cover losses you might incur, but don't buy more insurance than you need.
- ❖ Shop carefully for insurance, but don't let the cost of the premiums influence you to be underinsured.
- ❖ Review your insurance policies yearly to make sure that your risks are covered adequately for the price you can afford to pay.
- ❖ Be sure that you have enough in your cash reserves to cover emergencies that are not insured and be able to pay the deductibles if you have chosen to self-insure.
- ❖ Long-term care is not just for old people.

She Budgets

The money-smart woman knows that financial success doesn't just happen, it must be planned. Budgets, like diets, make most people tighten their jaws and dig in their heels. That is, until they come to see the benefits of it.

As I said in the opening chapter, you can customize all of this information and the techniques to your own style. If setting a budget is unpleasant to you, bring someone else into it with you. Schedule a time together. Work on a part of it at a time. Or, if you use a computer, let the computer assist you. Software programs like Quicken and

Money 2001 make it easy to set up your budget. They even ask you questions and make appropriate suggestions depending upon your answers.

The point is, you need a budget—or a "spending plan" for those of you who don't like the word "budget"—so you can confidently know you are making the most of your money. It is a discipline successful women learn.

It is difficult to make a suggestion for the way your income should be delegated because everyone has different needs. Plus, influences like the region you live in affect the amount you need to spend on housing. Also, the kind of work you do affects your clothing budget. Not only that, your leisure time activities can go from a good pair of hiking boots to season opera tickets.

One way to overcome this is to suggest percentages that each budget category might carry, for example:

❖ Housing: 25 percent to 30 percent

❖ Food: 8 percent to 15 percent

❖ Clothing and personal care: 6 percent to 8 percent

❖ Transportation: 5 percent to 10 percent

❖ Entertainment and vacations: 5 percent to 9 percent

❖ Insurance: 7 percent to 9 percent

❖ Healthcare: 5 percent to 7 percent

❖ Savings: 8 percent to 10 percent

How does your budget compare to these categories?

❖ Housing: _____ percent

❖ Food: _____ percent

❖ Clothing and personal care: _____ percent

❖ Transportation: _____ percent

❖ Entertainment and vacations: _____ percent

❖ Insurance: _____ percent

❖ Healthcare: _____ percent

❖ Savings: _____ percent

Once you get all these things in order, the next chapter will help you get more down on paper, and help you get even more organized.

The Bottom Line

When you are a money-smart woman, you manage your assets thoroughly and are dogged in your determination to understand your entire financial picture so you can make the most of it.

Reader's Journal:

Knowledge Gained:

_____

_____

_____

_____

_____

_____

_____

_____

_____

Steps I Will Take:

_____

_____

_____

_____

_____

_____

_____

_____

_____

Madeline (Omaha, Nebraska) believed she had a negative net worth. She considered herself a bad money manager and her mind took it from there. For years, Madeline and her husband avoided putting their actual financial situation on paper. She couldn't bear to see the truth for fear it would prove she was right.

Madeline's own children, grown and wanting their mother to face the financial challenge left by their father's death two years before, urged her to go through the financial planning process. In fact, her son went through it with her. He had a similar tendency to avoid financial responsibility.

Madeline and her son, John, enrolled in a financial planning class at a local community college. After the first class, Madeline was determined not to return. It felt too complicated. John wouldn't let her do it. By the third class, Madeline had broken through her resistance and was believing she could not only understand money but manage her own. In six weeks, Madeline and John had reversed their original condition and had their cash flow and net worth statements written out on paper.

All of Madeline's children were proud of her and the experience opened up a new level of conversation about money between them. Madeline credits her children with being brave enough to confront her about her negative money image and habits. She and John share a special bond and continue today meeting over coffee once a month for a financial check-up.

Chapter 8

Getting Your Debt Down—on Paper

The Bottom Line

When you discover how much money is coming in and going out of your budget, you can get control of your financial plan and destiny. The best way to get started is to get it down on paper, all of it.

Getting information about your income and expenses down on paper is the most important thing you can do because it shows you what comes in and what goes out. The more exact you are, the more information you have. The more information you have, the easier it will be for you to make adjustments in your spending and income.

While income and expense statements are not optional for the woman who wants to master her money, using the forms in this chapter are optional. You may prefer to create similar reports using software or another set of tools your planner provides. I offer it to you for your use and recommend you at least read through it to become familiar with the items you will need to have on hand to get a very clear picture of your financial situation. This would be a great project for a cozy weekend at home. Gather the items ahead of time so that once you sit down, you'll be prepared. Whatever you do, don't put it off.

Coaching Tip

I suggest that you do this as if it isn't your income and expense statement, so that you don't get emotionally involved and experience frustration, shame, or regrets. Knowing the truth gives you the freedom to make different choices.

If you already have your financial information recorded on a cash flow and net worth statement, I suggest you skim this chapter and then move on to the next. Another suggestion would be to get out your cash flow and net worth statements and study them to refresh your knowledge of where you are.

Your Income on Paper

Your income statement includes all the different ways that money can come into your budget. Enter your income on the following form:

Income Statement	Monthly	Yearly
Salary	_____	_____
Salary/spouse	_____	_____
Self employment income	_____	_____
Social Security	_____	_____
Social Security/ spouse	_____	_____
Pension	_____	_____
Pension/spouse	_____	_____
Rental income interest	_____	_____
Dividends	_____	_____
Capital gains	_____	_____
Spousal support	_____	_____

Income Statement	Monthly	Yearly
Child support	_____	_____
Other	_____	_____
Sub-totals	$_____	$_____

Your Fixed Expenses on Paper

Fixed expenses are those bills that if you didn't pay them, something would be shut off, discontinued, or cancelled. Enter your fixed expenses on the following form:

Fixed Expenses	Monthly	Yearly
Home Expenses		
Mortgage/rent	_____	_____
Homeowners fees	_____	_____
Real estate taxes	_____	_____
Special assessment	_____	_____
Home equity loan	_____	_____
2nd home expenses	_____	_____
Real estate taxes	_____	_____
Parking fees	_____	_____
Rubbish removal	_____	
Utilities		
Electric	_____	_____
Water	_____	_____
Oil	_____	_____
Gas	_____	_____
Telephone	_____	_____
Cell phone	_____	_____
Pager	_____	_____

(continued)

Fixed Expenses	Monthly	Yearly
Insurance		
Homeowners	_____	_____
Life	_____	_____
Disability	_____	_____
Health	_____	_____
Auto	_____	_____
Long-term care	_____	_____
Renter	_____	_____
Umbrella	_____	_____
Auto Expenses		
Loan payment	_____	_____
Insurance	_____	_____
Registration	_____	_____
License	_____	_____
Spousal and Child Support		
Spousal support	_____	_____
Child support	_____	_____
Work related		
Union dues	_____	_____
Other	_____	_____
Child Care		
Day care	_____	_____
Other	_____	_____
Sub-Total of Fixed Expenses	$_____	$_____

Your Variable Expenses on Paper

Variable expenses are those costs you may or may not pay every
month, and if you do pay them every month, the amount varies.
For example, you pay a dry cleaning bill monthly, but the amount
of the bill varies with the number of garments you have dry cleaned.

On the following grid, use the amount you spent last month, or average the amount you have spent the past six months.

Enter your variable expenses on the following grid:

Discretionary Expenses	Monthly	Yearly
Grounds Maintenance		
Lawn service	_____	_____
Supplies and equipment	_____	_____
Tree and shrub care	_____	_____
Other	_____	_____
Household		
Groceries	_____	_____
Cleaning supplies	_____	_____
Clothing		
Dry cleaning	_____	_____
Doctors		
Prescriptions/medications	_____	_____
Dentist	_____	_____
Other	_____	_____
Automotive		
Gasoline	_____	_____
Repairs and maintenance	_____	_____
Inspection	_____	_____
Tolls	_____	_____
Parking	_____	_____
Fines	_____	_____
Other	_____	_____
Transportation		
Bus	_____	_____
Train	_____	_____
Subway	_____	_____
Miscellaneous		
Continuing education	_____	_____
Baby-sitter	_____	_____

(continued)

Discretionary Expenses	Monthly	Yearly
Bank charge	_____	_____
Postage	_____	_____
Financial		
Tax preparation	_____	_____
Legal	_____	_____
Other	_____	_____
House Cleaning Expenses		
Weekly	_____	_____
Seasonal	_____	_____
Food		
Meals out	_____	_____
Coffee/snacks	_____	_____
Contributions		
Church	_____	_____
Charity donations	_____	_____
Other	_____	_____
Child Care		
Summer camp	_____	_____
Lessons	_____	_____
After-school activities	_____	_____
Vacations/Entertainment		
Vacations	_____	_____
Entertainment	_____	_____
Memberships/Dues		
Exercise/health clubs	_____	_____
Country/pool clubs	_____	_____
Kids' clubs	_____	_____
Other	_____	_____

Discretionary Expenses	Monthly	Yearly
Subscriptions		
Newspapers	_____	_____
Magazines	_____	_____
Gifts		
Birthdays	_____	_____
Anniversaries	_____	_____
Holidays	_____	_____
Personal Care		
Hair cuts	_____	_____
Manicures	_____	_____
Tanning salon	_____	_____
Toiletries	_____	_____
Massages	_____	_____
Other	_____	_____
Allowances		
Adults	_____	_____
Children	_____	_____
Miscellaneous		
Cable TV	_____	_____
Internet	_____	_____
Hobbies	_____	_____
Pet expenses	_____	_____
Other	_____	_____
Charge Cards/Loans		
1. _____	_____	_____
2. _____	_____	_____
3. _____	_____	_____
4. _____	_____	_____
5. _____	_____	_____

(continued)

Discretionary Expenses	Monthly	Yearly
Tax Expenses		
Federal	_____	_____
State	_____	_____
Local	_____	_____
Social Security	_____	_____
Medicare	_____	_____
Other	_____	_____
Sub-total variable expenses	$_____	$_____

Now, total your fixed and variable expenses and enter them here:

Total Expenses: $_____

Your Cash Flow Totals:

Total Annual Income: $_____ (Monthly: $_____)

Less Total Annual Expenses: $_____ (Monthly: $_____)

Monthly Cash Flow: (+ or –) $_____

Annual Cash Flow: (+ or –) $_____

If you are horrified to see how much you are spending, and how much you "piddle" away on what you consider stupid little things that are a waste in the general scheme of things, see what small action you can take to begin reversing the trend. But do not beat yourself up for this discovery.

Coaching Tip

If you are spending more than your monthly income, you are adding to your *debt*. Look at the "other" columns in your tables. If you are heavily weighted in those columns, you don't know where your money is going. Go back and see if you can figure that out.

We live in an acquisitive culture where we are brainwashed daily to want things we never knew we wanted before we saw or heard those ads. We live in a nation of overspenders. So while that doesn't make our overspending behavior okay (I'm a recovering overspender myself), it does make it understandable. The more compassion you have for yourself around the process, the more I trust that your changes and improvements will last, and not just be a temporary reaction to self-flagellation (beating yourself up psychologically).

Your Net Worth Statement

What are you worth in terms of money? Your net worth statement will reveal it. You may or may not have a positive net worth today. Many people don't. The point of this exercise is only to get the real facts on paper, much as a doctor does when she gets your medical history. Net worth is the value of your *assets* (what you own) minus your *liabilities* (what you owe).

Coaching Tip

I suggest you get as detached as possible from the figures you enter onto your net worth statement. Treat it as if it were someone else's so you don't get emotionally involved with the numbers. They are just numbers. They do not mean anything except to reveal the truth. The truth of your numbers can free you to change them, because you will really know what needs to be done instead of guessing.

Here's where the planning begins!

You'll have to do some homework here.

To determine your net worth you will first list all of your assets. Break these down into four categories:

❖ Real Estate Assets are your current home, vacation home, time shares, rental property, land, and any other real estate you may own.

❖ Current Assets (cash or cash equivalents) are assets that you can get your hands on within a short time. This is money that you expect to be able to use within the next year or two.

❖ Investment Assets are monies that you have invested for a long-term goal or a long-term gain. They can be turned into cash when the time is right and you plan to use the money for a goal you have made.

❖ Personal Use Assets are things that you use or treasure, which you may be able to sell if you need the money, but you don't plan to sell them to meet your financial goals. Unfortunately, some people's greatest treasures or family heirlooms have gone to pawn shops and disappeared into the general population because of desperation.

When you do your net worth statement, be sure that you write in the date when it was done so that you can see how far you have come the next time you revise it. Each revision will have a new date. Revise your net worth statement at least once a year so you can watch your progress.

Real Estate Assets

List your personal residence as a real estate asset. For example, how much do you owe on your mortgage? Call your mortgage lender and find out. You may be surprised at how much your original loan has shrunk. Then call a local real estate agent and ask her to do some comparisons of what houses similar to yours have sold for in your neighborhood. Don't use the valuation on which you pay your taxes. And don't bother to pay an appraiser. Real estate agents are usually happy that you recognize them out of the many who are selling real estate in your area. Besides, treating you well at this point may make you a client in the future or at least a good referral.

You will also list your vacation home, time shares, rental property, land, and any other real estate you may own. If you are renting, notice the benefit of owning your home to your net worth. For most people, home ownership is preferred, although renting has its place.

Real Estate Assets

Real Estate	Total	Self	Spouse	Joint
Residence	_____	_____	_____	_____
Vacation home	_____	_____	_____	_____
Time shares	_____	_____	_____	_____
Rental property	_____	_____	_____	_____
Land	_____	_____	_____	_____
Other	_____	_____	_____	_____
Real estate sub-totals	$_____	$_____	$_____	$_____

Current Assets

Current assets are cash and money that you can quickly get your hands on without a penalty or a tax consequence. Start with money in your wallet. Next list your checking accounts, savings accounts, and any short-term certificates of deposit (CDs). Then look for any cash value in your life insurance. If you have term insurance, there is no cash value, but if you have a permanent life insurance policy, call the company or your insurance agent and find out if it has cash value.

Current Assets

Current Assets	Total	Self	Spouse	Joint
Cash on hand				
Checking accounts				
Savings accounts				
Certificates of deposit				
Savings bonds/treasuries				
Money market accounts				
Money market mutual funds				
Cash value life insurance				
Other				
Current asset sub-totals	$	$	$	$

Investment Assets

Investment assets take time to convert to cash and you may have to pay a penalty for early withdrawal. They may also incur an income tax or a capital gain, which you would report to the IRS on your next tax return. Investment assets include stocks, bonds, mutual funds, treasury bills, and any tax-deferred retirement accounts such as 401(k) or 403(b) plans, IRAs, and annuities. You can call the companies to get your current balances, but this would be a good time to set up some files where you put your monthly, quarterly, and annual statements so that you can keep your net worth statement up-to-date and pleasantly watch it grow positively.

Investment Assets

Investment Assets	Total	Self	Spouse	Joint
Retirement Assets				
IRAs	_____	_____	_____	_____
Pensions	_____	_____	_____	_____
Deferred Compensation				
401(k)	_____	_____	_____	_____
SEP-IRA	_____	_____	_____	_____
Other	_____	_____	_____	_____
Annuities	_____	_____	_____	_____
Other	_____	_____	_____	_____
Business interests	_____	_____	_____	_____
Contracts	_____	_____	_____	_____
Other investments	_____	_____	_____	_____
Life insurance	_____	_____	_____	_____
Bonds	_____	_____	_____	_____
Stocks	_____	_____	_____	_____
Mutual funds	_____	_____	_____	_____
Government securities	_____	_____	_____	_____
Limited partnerships	_____	_____	_____	_____
Patents	_____	_____	_____	_____
Copyrights	_____	_____	_____	_____
Trusts	_____	_____	_____	_____
Personal loans to others	_____	_____	_____	_____
Investment real estate	_____	_____	_____	_____
Other	_____	_____	_____	_____
Investment sub-totals	$_____	$_____	$_____	$_____

Personal Use Assets

Here you will list things you use which have some value but would be difficult to convert to cash. Include automobiles, recreational vehicles and boats, home furnishings, collectibles, furs, jewelry, artwork, antiques, and so on.

Personal Use Assets

Personal Use Assets	Total	Self	Spouse	Joint
Automobile				
Recreation vehicles				
Personal property				
Jewelry				
Furniture				
Artwork				
Antiques				
Other				
Personal use sub-totals	$	$	$	$

Grand Total Assets

Now add up the value of your assets.

Total Assets

Your Assets	Total	Self	Spouse	Joint
Real Estate sub-totals	$	$	$	$
Current Asset sub-totals	$	$	$	$
Investment sub-totals	$	$	$	$
Personal Use sub-totals	$	$	$	$
Total assets	$	$	$	$
Grand total assets	$			

Are you surprised at how much you own (or don't own)? This is only one part of your net worth. The other part is to find out what you owe, and then we can find out what your net worth really is.

Your Liabilities on Paper

Now list your liabilities. These are what you owe.

Liabilities	Total	Self	Spouse	Joint
Automobile	_____	_____	_____	_____
Recreation vehicles	_____	_____	_____	_____
Education loans	_____	_____	_____	_____
Personal loans	_____	_____	_____	_____
Bank loans	_____	_____	_____	_____
Mortgages	_____	_____	_____	_____
Private residence	_____	_____	_____	_____
Vacation home	_____	_____	_____	_____
Rental property	_____	_____	_____	_____
Raw land	_____	_____	_____	_____
Home equity loans	_____	_____	_____	_____
Equity line of credit	_____	_____	_____	_____
Total liabilities	$_____	$_____	$_____	$_____
Grand total liabilities	$_____			

Now subtract what you owe (liabilities) from what you own (assets) and look at the result.

Grand Total Assets	$_____
+ Grand Total Liabilities	$_____
= Net Worth	$_____

If the answer is a negative number, don't despair. This is where the work begins. Your total debt (not including your home mortgage) should be less than 20 percent of your annual take-home pay. In other words, if you take home $30,000 per year, your debt should not exceed $6,000.

The Bottom Line

You can dance on your bottom line by deciding you are going to improve your net worth. Make a vow to yourself to become a positive net worth woman. The vow, along with specific plans and dates, will set things in motion for seeing the vow become reality.

Reader's Journal:

Knowledge Gained:

_____
_____
_____
_____
_____
_____
_____
_____
_____
_____

Steps I Will Take:

_____
_____
_____
_____
_____
_____
_____
_____
_____
_____

Cena (New York, New York) is an on-again, off-again spender. She loves bargain shopping, though she will pay $250 for a skirt at Saks. She is proud of the bargains she finds and feels a bit guilty for overspending, so much so that she often lies about what things cost, bragging to her friends about buying a blouse on sale when she actually paid full price.

Cena monitors her spending, sort of, in her head and budgets on a napkin. Her spending patterns are a result of her upbringing. Her parents gave her every opportunity they could afford, including full college tuition and a car upon graduation. She didn't have student loans or a car payment. While she was in college, Cena's mother co-signed a credit card for her. She was firm about Cena using it only for emergencies and then only when Cena knew she could pay off the balance each month. This arrangement worked, but as time went by, Cena got credit of her own and her spending became more cavalier and less cautious. She bought what she wanted when she wanted it.

The first few years out of college, Cena made a moderate salary and lived with roommates, used furniture, and a can opener in a mid-western city. Her erratic spending pattern continued, making things harder for her than they needed to be. Her behaviors resulted in a black hole when it came to saving and investing. She believed she didn't have enough money to put any away. As time went by and her career developed, she enrolled in her company's retirement plan, but only contributed the minimum. While she often thought about direct deposit into a savings account, she didn't ever do it.

Cena worked with a woman who was a smart spender. Cena took note. Their relationship was a good one and gradually Cena began following the example of her associate. She noticed she had more and more money at the end of the month. What impressed Cena the most was that her friend dressed well, enjoyed traveling and other niceties, and seemed to have a quiet confidence about her life, rather than Cena's more chaotic approach.

Cena's friend was a saver and investor, and Cena learned the value of both. She stepped into it slowly and found it every bit as satisfying to buy a mutual fund as a new blouse. Her life was revolutionized and so was her financial situation by becoming a smart spender. Yours can be, too.

Chapter 9

Spending Smarter

The Bottom Line

When you spend your money wisely, it can create more cash to put towards your plan for saving and investing. Anyone can do it.

Cena is not alone. Many women find themselves in the position of wanting to have nice things and live a comfortable life, and yet they are not focused on how they can spend now and save for their future at the same time. There are many simple things that the average person can do when it comes to spending. It's all a matter of making small adjustments in our money choices.

Commonsense Ways to Spend Smarter

There are many ways to spend smarter in your life. It's all about making minor adjustments in your behavior:

1. Consider getting a roommate to split your expenses.

2. If you have co-workers who live near you, carpool to save gas expenses and mileage/maintenance.

3. Do your own minor home improvements or repairs.

4. When making travel arrangements, check for discount tickets on Web sites such as travelocity.com or expedia.com.

5. Use coupons—even the millionaires do (how do you think they got to be millionaires?). These are especially good when grocery stores offer double or triple coupon days. Buy only things that are on the grocery list.

6. When you get tired of looking at your old furniture, don't buy new; refurnish and reupholster.

7. Even if you're shopping for one person, join a bulk-buying club to save on non-perishables such as toothpaste, batteries, soap, paper goods, and more.

8. Carry your lunch from home instead of always eating in a restaurant or cafeteria.

9. Look for two-for-one or "early bird" specials if you eat in restaurants with friends who are also trying to save more money.

10. Don't be too proud to ask for Senior Discounts or order from the children's menu if you find that restaurants serve you too much food.

11. Stop buying lattes or mochas every morning. Drink coffee at home.

12. Make your own frozen dinners.

13. Buy generic brands of food and drug store items.

14. Try to never buy groceries on your credit card.

15. Wash your own car and pump your own gas. Some gas stations even give free car washes with gas purchases.

16. Do you need a different car or will your old one still be fine for a few more years? Your insurance rate and licensing may go down as your car ages.

17. Talk to an insurance agent to see if you have the best rate for the age of your car.

18. If your old car is getting too expensive to maintain, buy a used car rather than a new one. The first two years of depreciation are the greatest.

19. Keep your car on its scheduled maintenance program so it will last longer.

20. Car pool to work or use city transportation and avoid parking costs.

21. Buy monthly passes for busses and trains.

22. Mow your own lawn. It's good for your mind, your body, and your pocketbook.

23. Clean your own house.

24. Use a library instead of buying books or magazines.

25. Check out movie rentals at the library; many of them are free.

26. Go to matinees to see new films.

27. Take enough cash from each paycheck to get you through that period and avoid too many stops at the ATM. Keep track of where that cash is going.

28. Pay off your credit card balances each month. Just paying the minimum will keep your credit clean but the interest continues to grow and you will find that the entire bill increases monthly even if you add no new purchases.

29. Refuse to pay an annual fee for your credit cards.

30. Never sign a credit card receipt without checking the purchase price(s). Those wonderful sale prices are not always scanned into the computer correctly.

31. Call your telephone long-distance carrier about every six months and ask if you are getting the best rate they offer for your kind of usage. They will often offer an unpublished rate just to keep your business. You can get comparative information on an Internet Web site called A Bell Tolls (www.abelltolls.com).

32. Do you really need cable TV? If you need it for good reception, just get the basic plan.

33. Look at your phone bill. Do you really need the extra line, caller ID, call waiting, and call forwarding?

34. Try e-mailing your friends instead of calling long distance.

35. Do you really need a cellular phone? If so, are you paying for a more expensive plan than you really need?

36. Review your insurance policies annually. Have enough insurance to cover your needs, but not more than what you need.

37. Check your insurance premiums. Get quotes online (www.Quotes.com) or from an insurance broker or agent to see if you can save some money on your premiums. You may get a better rate by having your home or renter's insurance with the same carrier as your auto insurance.

38. If you need life insurance, buy term insurance and be a responsible investor with the money you save over permanent insurance premiums. If no one is depending on you financially, you may not need life insurance at all.

39. Turn down your heat when you leave for the day to save on your heating bill.

40. Donate things you don't use or want to charity and use the receipts to help lower your tax bill.

41. Press your clothes at home if that's all they need, and save on your dry-cleaning bill.

42. Do you get the extended warranty on many things you buy? Sometimes that is covered by the store where you purchased the item.

43. Walk or ride your bike instead of joining a gym or having a personal trainer.

44. Shop for holidays all year long and take advantage of sales.

45. Instead of buying lottery tickets, put the money into your interest-bearing cash reserve account. Your odds of winning are better.

46. Save money in an interest-bearing account for big items like furniture and buy when you have the money instead of financing on credit.

47. If you buy a seldom-used item such as a kitchen appliance, purchase less than the top-of-the-line model or brand if it will serve you well enough.

48. Pay bills on time so that there are no late fees or interest added.

49. Research large items you plan to buy on the Internet to save gas, time, and avoid falling for persuasive sales people.

Be proud of the way you spend your money. If you feel guilty, find out where that feeling is coming from and work on it.

Coaching Tip

Memorize the closing dates of your cell phone bill and your credit cards. Manage your cash flow by waiting until the closing date to make more calls or charge something. I do this and it works great. I can really manage my bills.

Debit Cards

Debit cards, as you know, look just like credit cards. The difference is the payment comes directly out of your checking account instead of increasing your credit card balance.

When debit cards hit the scene, Cena was one of the first to trade in her old ATM card for the new, more convenient card. Her boyfriend was concerned about the safety of the debit card and was slower to get one. His concerns were shared by many who were concerned that using the card would enable someone to steal the card numbers and empty your checking account.

Most banks now have protection on their debit cards similar to that used by credit card companies. You will want to check with your bank to find out the protection your card carries.

Actually, debit cards have some real advantages to helping you be a smart spender.

❖ You can use the debit card instead of cash, reducing the amount of cash you need to carry and perhaps lose track of.

❖ Using the card means you don't have to use the ATM machine, which saves you ATM fees.

❖ When you use your debit card, you are given an option to get cash back. This again saves you from having to pay ATM fees.

❖ Using your debit card instead of your credit card keeps you from reckless spending on things you don't really need, because you know it will come directly out of your checking account.

❖ Using a debit card rather than a credit card will do wonderful things for your credit card balance. You will see the number of purchases decrease, making it possible to pay down your balance more quickly.

Buying Clothes

Smart spenders know that it's seldom necessary to pay full price for clothing anymore. With the proliferation of discount stores and weekly department store blowouts, virtually everything goes on sale soon after it even hits the racks. The next time you see a cute little black dress, ask yourself, do I need it today or tomorrow, or can I wait a few weeks to buy it on sale? I'm sure that most of the time your internal answer will undoubtedly be that you can wait. Waiting for that sale is spending smarter. It doesn't mean you're denying yourself the newest fashions, it just means you won't be the first one on the block to wear it.

Beyond department stores, there are many ways to spend smarter when it comes to clothing. Depending on your own style, you could be the perfect thrift shop customer. There are also consignment shops that often have expensive designer clothing at bargain basement prices. There are also discount chains and outlet malls that are great places for finding last season's items for really great prices.

Although it often is difficult to buy clothes online, there is a great discount design Web site that is worth visiting. At www.bluefly.com, you'll find the latest designer goods at up to 75 to 80 percent off suggested retail. It's a great place to shop for yourself as well as for gifts.

Review Your Options When Buying a Car

The most common questions about buying a car are:

 ❖ Should I lease or buy?
 ❖ Should I buy new or used?

The answers depend .... Assuming that a new car costs $22,000 (the national average at the time of this writing), you will want to explore all your options.

Leasing Your Car

Briefly, you may want to consider leasing a car if you:

1. Want to drive a new car every two or three years and want to keep your cash outlay at a minimum.
2. Drive less than 15,000 miles per year (even less for some luxury or sport-utility models). You will be charged up to 15 cents per mile over that limit.

3. You take good care of your car. Dogs who tear the seat covers and kids who spill juice are not considered "reasonable wear and tear" by car dealers. Small dents and scratches may also cost you at the end of the lease.

4. You use the car strictly for your business, which gives you a business deduction for it on your federal tax return.

But in order to make an informed decision about whether to buy or lease a car, you need to understand some of the nuances of each alternative. Here's a helpful chart about leasing. Also, check out www. autobytel.com, a great site you may want to visit when you're preparing to get a car.

	Lease	Loan
Terms	Lease terms are usually between two and four years.	Loan contracts are usually for a period of four to six years.
Type of vehicle	The shorter term and lower monthly payment of a lease agreement allow you to drive a new and more expensive vehicle every two to four years.	The higher monthly loan payments can make driving a new or expensive vehicle every two to four years impractical.
Ownership	You don't own the vehicle. You must make regular lease payments or risk losing the car. You must return it at the end of the lease, unless you decide to purchase it.	You own the vehicle.
	If you choose not to purchase the car at the end of the lease period, you are in the position of again leasing or buying another vehicle, but with nothing to "trade-in."	The lender holds a lien against the car. If you fail to make the loan payments, the lender can "seize" the car.

(continued)

	Lease	Loan
Upfront costs	Upfront costs usually include the first month's payment, a security deposit, a down payment, taxes, and registration fees. However, if you take into account the total cost of the vehicle and the monthly payment that you want, the sum is usually less than the upfront cost of purchasing.	Upfront costs usually include a down payment, taxes, registration, and other minor charges. This amount is generally larger than a lease payment for a comparable car, especially if your goal is a low monthly payment.
Monthly payments	Monthly payments are calculated based on the vehicle's depreciation during the lease term, rent charges, taxes, and other fees. Lease payments are usually lower than monthly loan payments.	Monthly loan payments are based on the total amount of the purchase price less the down payment, plus interest charges, taxes, and other fees. They are usually higher than monthly lease payments.
Insurance	The insurance premium is usually higher for a leased vehicle than for a comparable owned vehicle.	The insurance premium is usually lower than for a comparable leased vehicle.
Early termination	You are responsible for any early termination of your lease agreement prior to the full term of the lease. Charges for early termination are stipulated; on the lease contract. Make sure that you understand them.	You are responsible for paying off the loan.

	Lease	Loan
Vehicle return	You need to return the vehicle to the lessor at the end of the lease term. Check to see if there are end-of-lease charges.	You own the car. What you do with the car is entirely up to you.
Future value	The lessor bears the risk of the future market value of the vehicle.	If you decide to sell or trade in the vehicle at the end of the lean term, the risk of its future value is yours.
Maintenance	You are totally responsible for the maintenance of the vehicle during the lease term.	You are responsible for all maintenance of the vehicle.
Mileage	Most leases impose a limit on the total number of miles you can drive. You can negotiate a higher limit with the lessor at the start of the lease, keeping in mind that this will likely increase the total lease amount and monthly lease payments. Generally, there are extra charges if the actual mileage exceeds the contract limits.	No limit. The vehicle is yours. Drive it as you please. However, the higher the mileage, the lower the resale or trade-in value of your vehicle.
Excess wear	Similar to mileage restrictions, most leases limit the acceptable amount of wear to the vehicle during the lease term. If the lessor determines there is excess wear at the end of the lease period, expect to pay additional charges.	Like mileage, there is no limit on the wear of the vehicle. Again, the greater the wear, the lower the resale or trade-in value of your vehicle.

When it comes to spending smarter, leasing will probably mean you'll put less of an immediate dent in your cash flow. But the downside to that is the car is not yours at the end of the lease unless you buy it for the pre-determined residual value that you agreed to upfront when you leased the car. That means even if the car is worth less than the residual value at the end of your lease, if you want to buy that car, you'll pay the residual price and not the price that model may be selling for on the open market. Also, keep in mind there are stiff penalties for turning in the car before the end of the leasing period.

Buying Your Car

On the other hand, if driving the most expensive car you can afford is not a priority and would rather have your car payments go toward buying the car and owning it outright in a few years (and be payment-free!), then buying a car may be right for you.

The positive side of purchasing a car is that you'll have the flexibility of driving it as many miles as you please, and selling it whenever you want to. Build the payments into your budget or wait until you have saved up enough in an interest-bearing money market account to pay cash for your vehicle, or at least make a big down payment to reduce your monthly payments and dampen your monthly cash outflow.

Buying Used

If you're comfortable with purchasing a used car, it may be a smarter spending alternative. Often cars depreciate most rapidly in the first two years, so look at buying a good used two-year-old car with low mileage. If looks are important to you, see when the manufacturer last made a body change and buy one before the next model comes out.

Find out about pre-owned car warranties. These warranties usually are quite comprehensive. A good warranty can save you a substantial amount of money down the road if there's a mechanical problem with your used car. Also, keep in mind that in some states you have three days to change your mind after you have signed a contract—but not all states have laws like this. Call your local AAA office for the rules in your state.

Visit Web sites such as autobytel.com and Edmunds.com for information on new and used car values. You'll also find helpful calculators on those sites that can help you determine how much car you can afford as well as what your car payments may be, whether you lease or buy your car.

Buying a Car Online

If you are an Internet buff like I am, you may be able to spend smarter by purchasing your car online. Not only can you save money by making that purchase online, but you'll also save yourself a lot of time and energy.

To start your search, browse the Web sites of the auto manufacturers whose products you have an interest in purchasing. Most of these Web sites will let you "build" your own car, meaning you can add all the options and features you'd like on your car. Once you've determined what your ultimate driving machine is, visit www.edmunds.com or Kelly Blue Book's www.kbb.com to compare the invoice and MSRP (sticker price) for your car.

The three sites I found with the best prices for online car purchasing were www.carsdirect.com, www.autonation.com, and www.driveoff.com.

If you are looking for a used car, look at www.autotrader.com, which is the biggest used car Web site. You put in your zip code along with the model you want and Autotrader will tell you what's available in your area.

Expect to pay somewhere between invoice and MSRP for your car if you purchase it online. But don't be surprised if you can't do better than MSRP if the car you desire is a new model that is in demand. Also, luxury car dealers often will not bend on price, so you may be better off going directly to a local dealer if you're comfortable with the bargaining process. You may want to double-check prices with www.autoadvisor.com and www.carclub.com, which will give you regional selling prices for large metropolitan areas.

 Coaching Tip

A car is a big-ticket item that you will probably have for years. Saving money isn't the only criteria. I think buying a car you want is important. The idea is to select a car that you like and that is in the ballpark of your budget and go for it.

Review Your Options When Buying a Home

One area that many people overlook for finding ways to spend smarter is buying a home. When I was younger, I rented apartments as I moved to various cities because of my career. With each move I contemplated buying a home, because I hated the fact that the money I was paying in rent was the equivalent to washing it down the drain. At least if I had been paying a mortgage, I would have been building equity in my home as well as having the opportunity to deduct the interest payments from my income tax.

If you're settled enough in your life and have the money, consider purchasing a home because it is a great way of spending smarter. Think of it this way: When you rent a home or apartment from a landlord, you're paying *his* mortgage for *him* and helping *him* build equity. Turn the tables and spend your money smarter by being your own landlord.

Making Your Home Decision

A mortgage lender or real estate agent can help you calculate your mortgage payments based on current interest rates and the size of your down payment. There are also some good Internet sites to help you determine for yourself what you can afford to pay.

Go to sites like www.realtor.com, www.mortgagecalc.com, or www. financenter.com to see if you can afford a house right now—or if you need to wait until you have a larger down payment in order to decrease the monthly mortgage payment. Also refer to *The Complete Idiot's Guide to Buying and Selling a Home, Third Edition,* for more information on mortgages and qualifying for a loan. Plus, if you have Microsoft Office on your computer, you can go to Excel and use the automatic loan calculator.

Smart spenders choose their realtors carefully. A good one can save you thousands in reduced home price or in negotiating repair costs with the sellers. Make sure you interview real estate agents in the same manner as you would any other financial advisor. If you are buying a home, get a real estate agent to represent you as the buyer, so your interests are represented in the transaction. *Get an agent who will work strictly for you.* For help in finding one, contact the National Association of Exclusive Buyers Agents at 1-800-986-2322 or at www.naeba.org.

How do you know if your home will be a good long-term investment and truly a smarter way to spend your money? Consider the following tips when you are shopping for a new home:

Tip #1: Find a fixer-upper in a great neighborhood.

Tip #2: Do some research on what the best school system is in your area. Homes located in the vicinity of a strong school system usually hold their value better than those in areas with only average schools.

Tip #3: Location, location, location! Find the most house you can afford in the best location.

Remember, while your salary and your long-term debts would be used to determine what you could afford to pay for a house, there are other expenses connected with being a homeowner. In order to spend smarter, consider monthly costs you may have such as general upkeep expenses, monthly association fees, lawn maintenance, commuting costs, and those unexpected expenses that always hit you when you least expect them. If you do decide to spend smarter and purchase a home, keep your emergency reserve funded at all times.

Coaching Tip

I have heard that approximately 70 percent of homeowners use the standard deduction rather than itemizing their deductions. If you don't itemize, the homeowners deductions don't do you any good.

Calculating How Your Rent Compares to a Mortgage

If you currently rent and are considering buying a home, you can calculate what a mortgage payment might be in a comparable type of residence. You multiply the amount of your rent by 1.32. The answer is the amount you would pay for a home similar to what you are renting.

Your present rent	$_____
Multiply by 1.32	$_____
Equivalent monthly mortgage payment	*$_____*

This very rough estimate assumes that you are in the 28 percent tax bracket. If your tax bracket is higher, your tax savings will be correspondingly higher, but this gives you a ballpark figure to compare your monthly rent with a monthly mortgage payment including principle repayment, interest, homeowner's insurance, and property taxes.

Coaching Tip

You can lose money on your home, too, just like any other asset. Be careful in thinking you need a home because you don't want to throw money down the drain in rent. That could be a money myth if you don't do the research first.

Here's another way to determine whether buying a home or renting is better for you:

Comparing Rent vs. Buy

Line	Description	Rent	Buy
1	Annual mortgage payment	—	—
2	Annual real estate taxes	—	—
3	Annual upkeep	—	—
4	Total annual expenses (add lines 1, 2, and 3)	—	—
5	Amount of mortgage payment that is interest	—	—
6	Total tax-deductible expenses (add 2 and 5)	—	—
7	Tax savings (multiply line 6 by your tax rate of 15%, 28%, or 31%)	—	—
	Annual after-tax outlay (line 4 minus line 7)	—	—

The Rent column will have annual rent on line 1 and anything rent-relevant on line 3. Compare the totals you have in the Annual after-tax outlay line. Do you have that much in your cash flow? Which one fits you best financially? Which choice will be the smarter spending move for you to lower your cash outflow and give you extra cash to save or invest?

Negotiate for Fun and Profit

Another way to save some money is to learn to negotiate. Some of us are braver than others, but I have acquired some good negotiating skills over the years. Once you get the hang of it, it can be fun but, like sales, you have to be prepared to be turned down sometimes. It never hurts to ask!

I was furnishing some rental property (yes, a positive net worth woman can become a landlord if she wants to) at the same time my friend was furnishing an apartment for her daughter. We made a list of everything we needed to set up a kitchen. My friend watched ads in the Sunday newspaper, went to various stores, and bought a lot of things on sale. I spent the same amount of time three Saturday mornings and took my list to some neighborhood garage sales. We each completed our list, and she had spent over three hundred dollars while I spent less than $100. I had a lot of fun putting items together and making offers that were almost always accepted.

We usually think of negotiating prices on big items like cars and boats, but negotiation can be done with lots of things.

With two kids in college at the same time, I needed more cash flow than I could squeeze out of my budget, so I rented out our big house and moved into a small townhouse. The landlord said that I couldn't move in when I needed to because the painter would not be available for another two weeks and two rooms still needed to be painted. I offered to paint the rooms myself for $100 off the monthly rent. He agreed and I had that same discounted rent for two years.

As a landlord myself, I was always surprised that potential tenants didn't negotiate more with me. I always knew what my bottom line was and sometimes had to offer it to keep them from walking away because the rent was out of their budget. So, you see, negotiation can work both ways.

The Bottom Line

Spending smart creates more cash. More cash means more to invest or put toward the rest of your life plan. Anyone can become a smarter spender.

Reader's Journal:

What I learned:

_____

_____

_____

_____

_____

_____

_____

_____

_____

_____

Steps I Will Take:

_____

_____

_____

_____

_____

_____

_____

_____

_____

_____

Mary (New York, New York) grew up in a chaotic household where money was always a stressful issue. There was never enough money to go around, basic expenses were covered, but things other families regarded as necessary were not, and extras were out of the question. While Mary's family maintained a veneer of a middle-class life, she was often embarrassed to go to school because her clothes were all hand-me-downs. As a young teen, it was a constant trauma, she never felt like she fit in. There were years when a new back to school outfit was out of the question. Even winter coats and regular doctors' visits were not regular parts of their lives.

As soon as Mary could start working, she began buying basic necessities, like shampoo, school lunches, and new clothing for herself. She was proud of taking care of herself, but was also resentful that other teens spent their money on things they wanted and not things they needed. She always vowed that her children would never feel inferior and never go without.

When Mary had a family of her own she made sure her children had the trendiest clothes and the newest bikes. While Mary and her husband made adequate incomes and could afford these things for their children, they did not make enough to save as well. When Mary turned 40 she had a scare with breast cancer that made her step back and re-evaluate her lifestyle. For the first time she was faced with the knowledge that if something happened where either her husband or herself weren't able to work for a while, they would not be able to survive financially.

Mary turned out fine, but changed her whole outlook on finances by taking steps toward saving more and spending less. As to be expected, these changes didn't at first make her very popular with her children, but Mary knew that her children would one day understand. Mary opened up an IRA account, started contributing regularly to a stock account, and started a retirement plan.

Now that Mary is in retirement and needs no financial help from anyone, she looks back on that time of change and is grateful for the steps she took in securing her own financial future. Instead of being a burden on her children, as she would have been if things continued as they were, she now is able to support herself and has even set up a savings account for her grandchildren.

Chapter 10

Saving and Investing

The Bottom Line

Saving and investing while you pay off debt synchronizes your total cash and debt management effort, redeeming the time you need to build wealth and using the time you have to reduce debt. It's a good plan.

Some people might tell you to hold off saving and investing until your debt is paid down. I won't tell you that. I think it is self-defeating and maybe even depressing. Building assets is positive and optimistic; concentrating only on debt can make us feel stuck. Doing the two together is ideal. While you're filling your pot of assets, you're emptying your pot of bad debt. Then at some point the assets will outweigh the debts and you'll be a positive net worth woman.

While you're working your way out of debt, let some of your money work for you. This will allow you to get into the habit of saving and investing, even if you're only starting with a small amount each month. By the time you've finished paying off your debts, you'll already be in a great habit and be ready to increase your monthly amount that you can contribute to your savings and investment accounts.

My point is simply that you don't have to be completely out of debt before you begin saving. Getting your consumer debt out of the way will keep you from paying those high interest rates and worrying about whether the credit card rates will go up while you are still paying for last year's fashions. Your long-term loans, such as student loans and car loans, have a definite cut-off date when they will be paid, and you have a plan in your budget to pay them off on time.

Understanding the Difference Between Saving and Investing

Saving and investing are two different things. When you save you earn interest, when you invest, your money makes money. Saving is for the short term, investing is for the long term. Together, they keep you covered and prepared.

When it comes to saving, work toward putting enough money away so you have about three to six months of expenses in your savings account. It's considered an emergency fund and will pay for that unexpected engine repair or replacing the washing machine when it breaks down. Keep feeding the account so it maintains the balance. This is meant to protect you if you lose or quit your job and need time to find another one. An emergency fund of this size helps you sleep well at night because you know you are prepared for what might happen.

You will want quick access, without penalty, to this money, yet you want to earn as much interest on it as possible. So place your emergency fund in a money market fund, which is very safe. Money market accounts pay higher interest than savings accounts, so you will know your money will be parked in a fund that will keep growing at least with the rate of inflation.

Money markets are really mutual funds of cash investments like U.S. Treasury bills, CDs, and cash, and are managed by professional money managers. They pay more than bank savings accounts and often more than bank short-term CDs. They also allow you check-writing privileges. Some mutual fund companies that offer money market accounts will waive the initial investment for investors who set up a regular investment plan such as $25 or $50 per month.

Call several mutual fund companies to see if you can invest with them this way and compare the rates of return before you decide. You can find these rates in your newspaper or at www.bankrate.com.

Since you probably won't need all of your emergency reserve at one time, you may wish to buy some CDs of three to six months' duration. Choose several CDs with different maturities, or expirations, in order to avoid paying penalties for cashing them before their maturity dates. You can also buy CDs from stockbrokers. They may be able to find some with higher interest than your bank because they "shop" banks and find the best rates. Just be sure that the CDs you buy are FDIC insured.

Coaching Tip

Make sure you know the terms of any CDs you buy. Just like anything, they are changing. I have heard that you can actually have principle loss with a new type of CD called a Callable CD. Be careful with CDs, just as you would be with any other investment.

Get a Second Savings Account

In addition to saving for an emergency fund, it is also a good idea to continue to save in order to have cash that isn't invested in the stock or bond market. An old time stockbroker friend once said to me that it's important to save enough out of every paycheck until it hurts. He felt when someone starts saving like this, she'll start to curb her spending habits, and eventually it won't be as painful.

In fact, you won't even realize you're saving if you try the following:

❖ Direct deposit your paycheck. If you don't already have your paycheck directly deposited into your checking account, start now! By not having to go cash your check on payday, you will eliminate the impulse to put more cash in your pocketbook (which puts off saving).

❖ Order automatic savings withdrawal from your bank. Instruct your bank to make an automatic withdrawal of a set amount from your checking account, to a separate savings account at least once a month. By doing this, you won't even need to think about saving on a conscious level—it will automatically be done for you.

There are many ways to save money. Select the one that best fits your need for accessibility to your accounts, the interest you want to earn, and the amount you want to have in your account.

Long-Term Savings

Another extremely conservative investment for longer-term savings are EE Savings bonds. The interest is not very high on these and they are sold at a "discount." This means a $50 bond is sold for $25. The interest earned is free of state and local income taxes. You can buy them through banks or call 1-800-US-BONDS to learn more about them. Many experts feel these are too conservative to consider. It depends upon what you want and your level of risk tolerance.

Coaching Tip

Before you buy savings bonds, make sure you understand that they are very conservative investments and might not fit well into your portfolio.

Investing

While you're saving for your emergency reserve and your general savings account, you need to make money from your money. The way you do this is to invest.

There are many wonderful stories told of people with a low income investing to become millionaires. They discovered the secret of compounding. Some call compounding one of the wonders of the world, because it is so remarkable. Once your money starts compounding, or building upon itself, you start building wealth while you sleep.

It is shortsighted and old-thinking to believe you can create the money you need to live the life you plan—even a simple life—without investing. Investing is becoming an "everybody's" strategy, not just a rich person's strategy. It is the way to stay ahead of inflation and ahead of your plans.

Your 401(k)

One of the fastest ways to become an investor is to enroll in your company's 401(k) retirement plan at work. Most plans let you select your investment product from an assortment of options. This is a great way to step into investing and learn about the choices you have. From there, you can invest in other ways.

When you enroll in the 401(k), be sure to sign up for the deduction that will allow you to receive the company match, if your company has one. This means the company will match what you contribute each month. Consider it free money! If you don't do it (and too many people don't) you are leaving money on the table, tax-deferred money that will compound.

When you decide how much to put into your retirement plan, take advantage of the money that can go into it from your paycheck before taxes. This is called "qualified" money because it qualifies for tax deferral until you are 59½ (or you withdraw the money for other reasons that are allowed by the IRS). When you get a raise or a bonus, put what you can into your qualified retirement plan as long as you are not short-changing yourself or your family by doing so. If you have a workable budget, you won't miss that money. To find out how your 401(k) money will grow over time use the 401K calculator at www.womenswire.com (click on the Money area and the calculator is listed under the Tools section).

If you feel from time to time that you are saving too much for retirement, you can change your 401(k) contributions according to the rules of your employer's plan. Check your benefits book or talk to your human resources advisor about the plan. Human resources personnel are not allowed to give you investment advice but they can help you understand the company's retirement plan.

Coaching Tip

Your company puts effort into educating you about your 401(k) plan. Go to the employee meetings, listen and ask questions about anything you don't understand. It's your future and it matters.

IRAs

An Individual Retirement Account (IRA) is another tax-deferred opportunity available to those with earned incomes. If you don't work and are married, your spouse can contribute to an IRA for you. You can get a free booklet describing both the traditional and the Roth IRAs by calling any brokerage firm or mutual fund company, or by going online to any financial site.

The most comprehensive Web site I have found on retirement planning is www.investorguide.com (click on Retirement in the Personal Finance section). On it you will find explanations of all sorts of options as well as interactive calculators to help you with your planning.

Coaching Tip

Online is great, but there is nothing like a human being to help you. Once you've got the information from a Web site or from materials you read, find someone who knows about financial planning and discuss it. The numbers are the numbers. You need to make them come alive through the interpretation.

The trick to investing is to start early and invest at a high enough rate of return so that the money works as hard for you as you do for your money. While your emergency reserve should be invested very conservatively so that you can get at it easily, the longer you have until retirement, the more risk you will be able to take in your investment portfolio, depending on how well you can sleep at night knowing that the securities market goes up and down. Over time, though, the stock market has outperformed all other investments, but the caveat that you will read in every investment offering is "past performance is no guarantee of future results."

When I speak to women's groups, I often begin by asking how many in the audience consider themselves "investors." A few hands always go up. Then I ask, "How many have a retirement plan—401(k), 403(b) (for nonprofits), or IRAs." Nearly all hands go up.

Retirement plans such as 401(k)s are investments and need to be managed according to the time to retirement, just as taxable investments are managed. It is your money and your responsibility to keep it invested so that you will meet your retirement goals.

Learn the language of investing. Listen to financial reports, read the financial pages of the newspaper, and read some books on investing. Debbie Owens, another member of the Everywoman's Empowerment Team, has written an excellent guide called *Everywoman's Money: Confident Investing*. There are many other good books. Investing is a hot topic because it is the most proven way to build assets. The Internet also has some great resources such as www.financialmuse. com, www.cnbc.com, and www.smartmoney.com.

Whether your learning takes place from a book or on the Internet, do it at your own pace. After a while, you'll realize that what used to seem like a foreign language isn't that hard after all. Look around at those you know who invest, and you'll realize they are not any smarter than you, they've just learned how to do it. Once you learn, you'll realize it's a piece of cake.

Coaching Tip

Investing is easy to learn. I believe you can nearly learn it through osmosis, by simply reading the newspaper a few days a week. Read for understanding and you will be amazed at how much you learn over time. It's a kick!

Investment Clubs

Since we know that women like to work in groups, one way to learn about investing is to join an investment club. If there are no investment clubs where you live, get some friends together and start one.

Coaching Tip

Gather like-minded people together for your investment club. People get funny about money. If you are a risk taker, you might think twice about inviting a friend who has all of her money in CDs. Education goes a long way, but still you want to be able to reach consensus without too much conflict.

The National Association of Investors Corporation Web site at www.better-investing.org gives lots of information on investment clubs. The site contains complete instructions for organizing and operating an investment club. You may also consider purchasing the *NAIC's Official Guide: Starting and Running a Profitable Investment Club.* By following this book's suggestions you will learn how to organize your club easily and properly. Along the way, you will become a better investor. The book includes a sample partnership agreement and instructions for starting an investment club.

The Bottom Line

You can fund your life plans most effectively through a systematic savings and investment program, supplemented by an aggressive debt-reduction plan.

Reader's Journal:

Knowledge Gained:

_____
_____
_____
_____
_____
_____
_____
_____
_____
_____

Steps I Will Take:

_____
_____
_____
_____
_____
_____
_____
_____
_____
_____

If you had asked Allie to paint a picture of her life today, she would not have been able to do it. Fresh off a divorce after 14 years of marriage to a very wealthy man, Allie told herself she would return to the kind of life she had lived prior to her marriage—simple and predictable.

She had cultivated a reputation in her metropolitan city as a successful and artistic set designer in the local arts community, a position she continued after the divorce. She moved into a small townhouse outside town, trimmed her lifestyle, and worked to re-establish herself on her own again.

Allie visited a financial planner because she had received some 401(k) money from the divorce. The planner, an intuitive professional, sensed that Allie was moving backward, not ahead. She felt Allie was thinking small, rather than large. Although she did not say so, Allie felt a large life could only happen if she were married. Over time, the planner helped her see that she was limiting her life with limiting beliefs.

Allie was resistant to doing a financial plan because she didn't want to face what she might see. She was afraid she wouldn't be able to pay her bills and pay off her $9,000 credit card debt. However, Allie faced her fear, and the process gave her new confidence to take charge of her life at a new level. Her bravery has led to other developments.

Allie committed to following her financial plan to the letter. Soon after her vow to get out of debt and build her own wealth, Allie was offered a wonderful and lucrative artistic project. It could be done on the side without sacrificing her current job. Shortly after that, another offer came that was even more profitable requiring even less effort. Her earnings on her side jobs equaled well over $100,000 a year.

Allie began to see herself and her possibilities differently. She is realizing that she, too, can create what she calls a "large" life, meaning she can fill it with people and adventures that thrill her. Recently, Allie called her financial planner and said, "Guess where I just came from!" She had flown to Europe with a friend of hers who was a department store buyer. The real news was that she flew there on free miles she had earned while married. "I didn't know I had over 100,000 miles because for some reason I was afraid to open the account to see what was there." She added, "I'm realizing I can fly anywhere. In fact, I'm realizing I can do anything I set my mind to." Go, Allie!

Chapter 11

Upping Your Income

Spending less is one way to get more cash. Upping your income is the other way. Doing both is best. Spending less frees up money and earning more brings in more money. When you have more money, you have more opportunities to live, give, save, and invest. More opportunities mean a fuller life for you and those you love. It also means you will be able to stay in charge of your choices longer.

There are several ways to increase your income:

- ❖ Earn more at your present job.
- ❖ Change jobs.
- ❖ Get a second job.
- ❖ Increase your skills through education.
- ❖ Start your own business.

We will look at each of these methods of upping your income, but first ask yourself how much more you are planning to earn and give yourself a realistic deadline for earning it. This is an important part of the process of bringing more money into your life. It nails down specifics and sets you on a course that is real, rather than wishful thinking.

Write your intention here:

I intend to earn $_____ more than I do now, and I intend to do it by _____. Today's date is _____. Now, write out this intention in other places where you will see it so you will keep your vow in mind.

Coaching Tip

In all my years of helping people manage their money, I have never seen someone set an intention to earn more money by a certain date and not have it happen. There is something to the notion that declaring an intention and following it up with action results in the intention becoming the new reality. As your coach, I urge you to do it. Reach one milestone, and then make a new intention for the next milestone.

Let's look at each of these methods for increasing your income.

Earn More at Your Present Job

Many women are under-earners; they get paid less than they deserve for the work they do, and often less than their male counterparts. In fact, women still earn about 24 percent less than men. Regardless, there are ways to get a raise and put yourself on a career-building path with new momentum.

First, I've distilled some guidelines for you from experts on getting a raise:

❖ Understand the process of raises in your company.

❖ Know your job description. You may be performing at a level beyond your job description, making it easy to prove your point.

❖ Be familiar with what others make in comparable companies. Check with professional associations for surveys of members' salaries.

❖ Help the boss know you do good work on an ongoing basis. Pass along notes or e-mails of praise from others, as well as copies of projects you have completed.

❖ Put in extra effort, take appropriate initiative, and make a list of how you have contributed beyond what you were hired to do.

❖ Prepare to present a brief summary of your positive contributions to the company. Rehearse it, don't memorize it, and present in a relaxed voice.

❖ Time your request to coincide with a positive accomplishment or review.

❖ Document your reasons for believing you deserve the raise.

❖ Be prepared to name the amount of raise, or what range, you want.

❖ Practice your pitch out loud, alone, and with someone.

❖ If the answer is "no," find out why. Get a written reason, if possible, then get busy meeting that requirement and document it.

In the meantime, do your research. If you don't know what your company's policy is for increasing salaries, find out. What percentage of a raise is normal? What is the typical process of obtaining a raise at your company? Take a class on negotiating or read a book and practice with a friend or member of your family.

I suggest you keep a running log of your accomplishments. In a notebook or on your computer, record the projects or tasks you have done, particularly those that represent extra effort or unique contribution. Show how you have overcome challenges, and be specific about your role in them. Don't inflate your contribution, but don't understate it either.

And, remember, bosses expect to be asked for raises. Be up front and direct. Say, "I'd like 15 minutes of your time on Thursday to discuss my salary and position."

When you make the request, know that your boss may have to get approval from someone else to give you the raise. Give her plenty of ammunition to lobby for your raise to her supervisor. Be open to other alternatives, like an adjusted work schedule, more time off, being assigned to a project with a bonus.

I can tell you that in most cases, managers want to reward excellence. They are even *eager* to do it. So be sure you are excellent, not only in your work, but that you put yourself on a continual learning curve to be a growing, mature person behind the job. Don't settle for mediocrity or let your peers be your standard of performance. Look higher.

The following is a list of the 20 leading occupations of employed women (16 years of age and over).

Occupation	Percent Women in That Occupation
Secretaries	98.6
Managers and administrators	30.5
Cashiers	77.0
Sales supervisors and proprietors	40.9
Registered nurses	92.9
Sales workers, retail, and personal services	63.9
Nursing aides, orderlies, and attendants	89.9
Elementary schoolteachers	83.8
Bookkeepers, accounting, and auditing clerks	91.4
Waiters and waitresses	77.4
Receptionists	95.5
Accountants and auditors	58.6
Sales workers, other commodities	67.8
Cooks	44.0
Machine operators, assorted materials	32.6
Investigators and adjusters, excluding insurance	77.3
Secondary schoolteachers	57.5
Administrative support occupations	79.2
Janitors and cleaners	35.8
Hairdressers and cosmetologists	90.8

Change Jobs

If you determine that you cannot thrive financially in your existing job, you may want to move on, either within the company you work for now or in another one.

Here are some tips for changing jobs:

- ❖ Prepare carefully.
- ❖ Quietly explore other options.
- ❖ Determine if you want to stay in the same profession or move to another one.
- ❖ Let trusted friends and/or associates know what you are thinking. Enlist their help in networking.
- ❖ If you want to stay with the same company, pay attention to other departments. Note managers with a positive reputation and staff.
- ❖ Find out the direction your company is going and get in on it.
- ❖ Educate yourself on other companies, what they pay, and how you might fit in.
- ❖ Visit online employment facilitators like www.monster.com or www.headhunter.net.
- ❖ Ask your financial advisor how to handle the financial side of leaving.
- ❖ Look behind your job description to the skills you use in carrying it out. Sell the skills on your resumé.

There are some excellent resources to help you explore your possibilities. One online resource that I found helpful is Career Search from College Board online at www.collegeboard.org/career. They offer helpful information and assessments at no charge.

Think out of the Box

Many women are moving to nontraditional jobs like construction to up their income. They find the work refreshing and their pay instantly improved. For information, visit the Reference Librarian at your local library or go online and do a search using the key words "nontraditional employment, women." There are organizations across the country helping women find nontraditional employment.

When making a career decision, head for the top: the top-paying field for your skill set at a top-rated, female-friendly company. You've got to work somewhere, so work with the best. Also, find out what fields are emerging with the greatest strength in the next 10 years and get yourself in on the explosion, even if means getting special training.

And don't forget to consider work in the area of your greatest passion. If you are a computer expert and you love music, put the two together. From studio production to concert tours to logistics, there is plenty of room for someone who's good at computers.

Get a job that pays you more than you make now in a field you love and/or at a company that takes good care of its female employees. It takes courage to move forward, but it also takes courage of a different kind to stay put and risk having enough. Choose your courage, but keep your risk calculated. Pave the way for every move you make so you reduce or eliminate the actual amount of risk.

Nothing Has to Be Forever

If you do decide to change jobs, there are some basic things to consider besides just going to another company that will pay you more money. Be sure that this is what you want to do for yourself. If you are extremely happy where you are but you need more money, you could ask for more opportunities within the company.

Some of the best advice my mother ever gave me is "Nothing has to be forever. Go with what seems best at the time, and be willing to make changes when it feels right to make them." As a result I have had six careers so far, and they have all built on each other.

My degree is in Family and Consumer Science. My first career was as a home economist for the Iowa State University Extension service. In that job I designed and presented programs on new homemaking information. Another facet of my job was teaching women to help girls learn homemaking skills, community leadership, self-esteem, and team-building through their local 4-H clubs. This led to an opportunity to work with 4-H leaders in Sweden.

My next career was to apply what I had learned as a full-time homemaker—mother of two kids and wife of an IBM computer programmer whose career kept us moving to a new community every few years. Since I was trained as a teacher, I developed some interesting opportunities for myself by creating and teaching women a variety of courses through adult education programs and working with developmentally handicapped children to help them learn some basic work skills for the food service industry.

My kids were 11 and 12 when my husband died and I had to put my skills into high gear and become the family's breadwinner. I sold high-tech office equipment to businesses in New York. Sound unrelated?

Not necessarily. Human relations people have told me that teachers very often make great sales people because they are organized, can think on their feet, and are used to working hard. While my kids were in college and I was traveling throughout the country as a National Account Manager, I spent my airplane time studying financial planning through self-study courses.

This led to my sixth career, as a certified financial planner, where I specialize in working with women. My friend Kristen even cross-stitched and framed a picture that she designed. It says "Financial Therapist" and is proudly displayed in my office. More than once it has broken the ice with a new client. It is in green, of course.

I feel as though I have come full circle in my passion for teaching women. And I'm able to share my mother's wonderful advice that "Nothing has to be forever."

Look at Where Your Company Is Going

If you hear rumblings about it being sold or closing or laying workers off, don't spend your energy grumbling about it in the cafeteria or whispering in your cubicle. Instead, quietly start to network yourself with people in your area of interest outside your present company. Join a professional organization and go to some meetings. Or get to know people who hire consultants in the field you want to work in.

Polish up your resumé and go to the nearest copy shop. If someone sees you copying your resumé at work, your secret will be out. Imagine that you are the manager and you see someone's resumé has been left on the platen glass of the department copier!

If you do leave, be sure to leave in good graces. You will be happy that you didn't bad-mouth the company, or the people who work there, before you decided to leave. You never know, they may be working for you someday! Let your manager know that working there has been an enjoyable experience and you have learned a lot, but you feel that it is time to move on and do something that will fit you better at this time.

If you want to work part-time, job sharing is becoming more and more popular. Employers find that mothers with small children are good candidates for job-sharing. If you can be matched up with someone with the same skills and work ethic as yours (with an opposite time frame for the job), the employer may get 60 hours of work from two people.

Changing jobs is more common today than ever before. You've read that the average employee makes seven career changes in her professional life. Changing careers is also becoming quite common. Before you make the move, prepare the way. Know what you're going to do and when. It is not in your best interest to get caught in someone else's delays and postponed plans.

Before You Leave

Before you start looking for another job, know your company's benefits. If you have lost your benefits book, ask the human resources department for a new one.

When is profit sharing given out? Don't leave just before that happens and miss out on your share of the profits to which you have contributed with your good work.

Don't leave on December 24 if you are just about to be given several holidays off at the end of the year. You've earned them, and you won't get paid for them. If you leave, will you get paid for the vacation you haven't taken? If not, take the vacation first, then leave.

What about vesting? Leaving a few months before you are vested to receive a retirement pension (even if you aren't old enough to collect it yet) is like getting a divorce after you have been married nine years and eight months, and you may have just given away some social security benefits because the marriage didn't last for ten years.

Protect Your Retirement Plan

Get a copy of your most recent retirement contributions. Go over them carefully, make sure that everything you have contributed is in your account, and note your company match is included, if it is offered.

When you leave, don't touch that money! You will have some choices. Your former company may allow you to keep the money in their plan, and your new company may allow you to bring it with you. You need to know which company has the best plan for you. Another option is to have it rolled over into your own traditional IRA. Before you make a decision, discuss this with a financial planner to help you determine what is best for you. At any rate, don't have the money transferred directly to you. If you are not sure, leave it where it is until you have made a well-thought-out decision.

If you take the money before you are 59½, you must pay the tax on the entire amount plus a 10 percent penalty for taking it out too early. There are some exceptions to this, and you should contact a financial planner, an accountant, or the IRS directly to see what the latest legislation allows and whether or not you are eligible. If you are 59½ or more, you will still be responsible for the tax on the amount you withdraw but there is no penalty.

You may hear that you can have the money for 60 days and then put an equal amount into a new retirement account. If you do this, your old company will deduct 20 percent to give to the Internal Revenue Service, and you will have to claim it back on your next tax return. It isn't worth all that paperwork unless you absolutely need to give yourself a 60-day loan and you know for sure where the money will come from before the 60 days are up. There are much better ways to give yourself a loan.

Medical Benefits

Your benefits book should tell you explicitly how the company's medical benefits work. If it is not clear to you, ask the human resources person to explain them. By law, your current employer must give you an opportunity to continue to be on their medical plan at your own expense for a determined amount of time. At this writing, the length of time for coverage is up to 18 months.

Before you take a job with another company, ask to see their benefits book. You won't want to ask for it on the first interview; wait until they offer the job. This would be especially important if they have exclusions on pre-existing medical conditions. If you have any of those conditions, don't take the job until you have found medical insurance for yourself.

Age Myth

Some women over 50 are concerned that employers will overlook them because of their age. Let's break that myth right now. Employers are looking for people with good work ethics, and you may be just the one they are looking for. In fact, many prefer the maturity and reliability of seasoned women.

The Federal Age Discrimination in Employment Act prohibits firms with at least 20 workers from considering age in hiring, firing, promoting, demoting, or compensation. However, it is sometimes hard to prove that you were discriminated against for any of those reasons.

If you have structured your resumé well, an interviewer may be surprised at your age when you appear. If you know that you had all of the qualifications and you proved yourself in the interview (but you did not receive an offer), ask the human resources person in charge of your case for feedback on why you were not offered the job. This is especially important if you find out later who did receive offers for the position.

This happened to me in an interview. I asked for the feedback so that I could use the information in future job applications and interviews. I had to ask for the feedback periodically for two months, but I was relentless and finally I did get something that I felt was an answer to keep the company in compliance with the Age Discrimination in Employment Act. Although I was on to bigger and better things by then and had neither the interest nor the energy to sue for my rights, I wanted the company to realize that we don't take these excuses lying down and we can protect others by insisting that the law is enforced.

According to the U.S. Department of labor, 39 percent of the workforce was 40 or over in 1997 and by 2006, 52 percent of the workforce will be over 40. Because of the low unemployment rate in this country and the types of jobs that must be filled, if employers don't hire older people, they will have trouble filling the positions.

Get a Second Job

More and more people are working more than one job. It's a fast way to fund something specific and to pay down credit card debt. Second jobs seem to work best when they are very different from your full-time job. Many experts also recommend you put a time limit on the second job to prevent a sense of forever, unless of course you are inspired by the job.

Usually people take on second jobs to pay for holiday gifts or vacations. Frequently, however, it is to supplement the existing income and pay for monthly expenses. As you pay down your debt, you will have more income. At that point, you can decide to continue working and using your supplemental income to fund an IRA or retirement plan, or quit moonlighting.

The most popular second jobs are in fast food. You may want to think beyond that to activities that are fun to you. Assist with hot air balloon rides, groom and walk horses, run errands while you're out anyway, cook and freeze low fat meals for friends, present tea parties for six-year-old girls. You name it.

Coaching Tip

Imagine working part-time for four months and putting all of that money toward paying down your credit cards. Or, if you don't have debt but not enough income to fund serious investing, use your part-time income to invest. You'll be amazed at how quickly you will move forward financially. Try it!

Increase Your Skills Set Through Education

If you choose to earn more cash by staying at the company currently employing you, check into in-house training programs. Many companies today actually help pay for the college and/or graduate studies of selected employees. Tell your supervisor you want all the special training you qualify for, and then be an excellent student who makes your tuition a good company investment.

You may decide you want to return to school part- or full-time on your own. Half of the students enrolled in college programs across the country are 25 are older. A woman I met recently had returned to school at 60. She said, "It was great. I didn't realize how smart I'd gotten just by living this long!"

If you dream of going back to school, do it. There are many good scholarships and loans available for people of all ages. Look at www.finaid.com, www.fastweb.com, or www.collegeboard.org to find out where there is financial help for you to meet your educational goals. You can also call The College Board at 212-713-8165 and ask for publications on financial and nonfinancial college planning issues. The Federal Student Aid Information Center (1-800-433-3243) offers information about federal grants, loans, and the financial aid process.

Loans are available for students with good credit history, which is another reason for working quickly to clean yours up, if necessary.

You may need to take the high school equivalency exam if you didn't graduate from high school, and if you want to go to graduate school, you may have to take the GMAT exam. Women do both of these things every day. You can, too. Call your local department of education or a local college to find out where these tests are given.

We all want our children to get the education they deserve. You deserve the same. Perhaps spending some money on education for yourself would help you to contribute to theirs in the long run if you choose to help them. The more you have put away for them, the less financial aid they will receive. I'm not saying that you shouldn't be saving now for your kids' college funding, but they may be as responsible for helping to fund their education as you are for yours.

Going back to school will require a lot out of you, especially if you're also going to be working. If you have a family, get their buy-in for the short-term life adjustments. Show them how it will be worth it for everyone.

Today, your choices for higher education are vast. You can learn online and receive your degree, you can attend college one weekend a month for two years, or you can go the traditional route on campus. The point is this, college graduates usually earn more than noncollege graduates in the typical workplace. Your investment in education, in other words, will likely pay off very well and can be considered a valuable investment in yourself.

You may wonder why I would recommend going to college when I am also encouraging you to get out of debt. Education is not consumer debt, it is "good debt." A school loan, if you need one, will temporarily reduce your net worth, but it will ultimately increase it.

Start Your Own Business

Some business owners would chuckle to see a section like this included in a chapter about earning more income. For many business owners, owning a company means not having an income for sometimes two or more years. Of course, if the business survives and makes a profit, the payoff will be worth it. If not, it can mean a devastating loss in both income and net worth.

The truth is, however, that business owners do have the greatest chance for high net worth. If you have always wanted to own your own company, be sure that you can afford to do it. Take each step carefully and calculate your risk along the way.

There is a great deal of help available to you if you are going to start a business. Small Business Development Centers are located throughout the country, and they are joined by a multitude of live and online resources. There are also numerous organizations created especially for the woman-owned business, including the Business Women's Network (www.bwni.com) and the National Foundation for Women Owned Businesses (www.nfwob.com).

Remember, starting your own business can be as simple as turning the Christmas toffee you make once a year into a cottage candy company. Or it can be as logical as turning your new van into an airport shuttle or a guided tour van for points of interest in your area.

Or, you may prefer to use your talent at the piano to teach piano lessons. Maybe you love children and want to host an after-school study program at your home for kids in your neighborhood.

Ask yourself what logical outgrowth of who you are and what you do could be transformed, or monetized, into an income stream. Let it develop naturally, and pay yourself first.

Before you open your doors, get some books from the library and develop a good business plan. Talk to people who are in the business and ask what they recommend for you.

Don't give up easily on pursuing the possibilities of having your own business if you really feel strongly about doing it. Choose a business that comes naturally to you, that uses your best skills. Just be sure that you have done as much research as you need to before you plunge in. Remember, you are trying to increase your net worth through this venture.

Coaching Tip

Well over half of all new small businesses fail. A disproportionate amount of the debt wiped out in personal bankruptcy cases comes from personal liability on small business debt, according to the U.S. Small Business Administration (myvesta.org).

So, whether you are opening a franchise, starting an Internet business, or launching a delivery service, do it right. Listen to those who have been there. Take advantage of every class and resource, and remember that the Internet can give you as much information in three hours as you could possibly want. An online excursion to flametree.com will get you started.

Be a money-smart business owner and watch out for your own bottom line. No business is worth losing your net worth.

Coaching Tip

When you own your own business, you are essentially in marketing and sales. If you don't like to sell, you might be better off working for a company that employs people who do. Also, you need to do the work of the business owner every day. Between marketing/sales and administration, there isn't too much time left to provide the product or service to your customers or clients. That's why business owners work such long hours. I've been self-employed for years and I love it. I work longer hours for less money than when I was in the corporate world, but I wouldn't trade it.

The Bottom Line

If you need to increase your income, do it. Put your best ability to make things happen behind your choice to have enough. Adjust when necessary, but don't turn back.

Reader's Journal:

Knowledge Gained:

_____

_____

_____

_____

_____

_____

_____

_____

_____

_____

_____

Steps I Will Take:

_____

_____

_____

_____

_____

_____

_____

_____

_____

_____

_____

Marge (Miami, Florida) was preparing for retirement. She and her husband had found their dream home in sunny Miami and were finally going to be leaving the cold winters of New England behind. Believing she had what most would call perfect credit, she had assumed the loan process to be a quick formality and was busily packing up her house when the call had come in that she had been denied the loan. Flabbergasted, she said nothing as the loan officer politely explained that this decision was made on her low credit score. When her husband returned home that evening they sat down and wrote letters asking for copies of their credit report. As they wrote they rehearsed every possible thing in their past that might have caused this denial, and could think of nothing.

When the credit report finally arrived, it did not take long for Marge to realize what had happened. You see, Marge's mother and daughter are also named Marge, as part of an old family tradition. So any credit mistakes, credit inquiries, and so on that her mother and daughter had made over the years had been mistakenly put on Marge's credit report.

After many letters and phone calls to the mortgage company and credit bureaus, Marge's credit report was cleaned up and she was granted the loan. If Marge had annually reviewed her credit report, she would have been aware of these potential problems and taken steps to rectify them. Because Marge had not once looked at her credit report before this problem, there was an accumulated list of errors that took weeks to rectify.

Chapter 12

Protecting Your Cash and Credit

The Bottom Line

Putting a security system, so to speak, around your cash and credit is every bit as good an idea as installing a system in your home or car. After all, it's your cash, and it's the ability to borrow that buys the home and car.

Protecting what you are building in the way of assets and credit history is smart, and the energy and creativity you put into it is worth it. There is a fine line between being overly fearful about using the many conveniences available to us today and being cavalier about believing such a loss would ever happen to you. You will want to find the balance.

The other day a friend of mine said her debit card number was stolen over the phone by an order taker at an online catalog company. The young girl on the other end of the phone had cleverly used the debit card information to purchase a number of items in the $25 to $50 range, easily overlooked on a billing statement. Once caught, she confessed to doing it to a number of customers. My friend's total loss was several hundred dollars. Almost every day, we hear similar stories.

Just as you work to protect your name and reputation in business, you must work to protect your assets and credit history as a person. There are a number of threats to both your cash and credit history in this day of technology, travel, growing populations, and mounting assets, but there are also some proactive measures you can take to keep those threats at a distance.

Understanding Your Credit History

There are several things to protect in your financial life, and your credit history is right up there at the top. In many ways, it is your ticket to play or not play in the world of asset and debt management.

The Fair Credit Reporting Act (FCRA) was designed to promote privacy and accuracy of information contained in your credit report. In effect, it was designed to put you, and not the credit bureaus, in control of information that affects your credit life. Your credit report determines your ability to get credit and the terms of the credit. Without an accurate credit report, your ability to get credit can be greatly impaired. The FCRA is a government regulatory agency that protects you and your credit. The FCRA has many provisions to do this. Provisions contained in the FCRA include:

❖ You are entitled to know and dispute any information contained in your credit file.

❖ A Credit Reporting Agency (CRA) must take action by correcting or deleting information that is inaccurate or unverified within 30 days of the dispute.

❖ A CRA cannot report damaging information that is more then seven years old, except in case of bankruptcies, which may be reported for up to 10 years.

❖ The FCRA limits access to your credit report to companies or individuals recognized by the FCRA.

If a Credit Reporting Agency violates any of the above provisions, you as the consumer are entitled to seek damages in court. The Federal Trade Commission says that inaccurate credit reports are the number-one source of consumer complaints, and they can take several months to resolve.

Credit Scoring

Consumers like you who seek a home mortgage, auto loan, or credit card are assigned a credit score. A credit score measures the relative degree of risk of delinquency or default that you represent to a creditor or lender. The score is also called a "risk score" and is based on information in your credit report and also on information about how other people with similar information have repaid their bills. These scores are widely used by lenders for mortgages and auto loans, and credit card companies in evaluating loan applications.

This credit score, in combination with a variety of other types of information including outstanding debt and income, will determine how good of a credit risk you are. The credit score most commonly used is the FICO score developed by Fair, Issac & Co. in the 1960s.

The FICO score is based on a number of factors, such as your consistency in paying bills on time, the number of credit cards you have, the balances that are carried, and a number of other factors. The FICO score is used by lenders to make billions of credit decisions every year. The scores range from 300 to 900 with the average score being in the 600s and 700s. There is no set score that you have to have to get credit. It is purely left up to the discretion of the lender to decide what level of risk they are willing to accept in giving you credit.

Credit Scoring Model

To develop a credit scoring model, random loan customers are sampled statistically to identify characteristics that relate to patterns of repayment. Then, each of these characteristics is assigned a weight based on how strong a predictor it is of the likelihood of repayment. The higher the score, the lower the risk for the lender. A borrower with a score of 660 or greater is considered to be of less risk for the lender, while a score of 620 or lower is a poor credit score. Credit scoring cannot rely on factors such as race, religion, gender, income, address, employment, national origin, or marital status, but some scoring systems may use age as a factor in determining a credit score.

Credit scores rely on the following:

❖ Occupation and time at present job.

❖ If you are a homeowner.

❖ Past payment performance. A pattern of late payments brings down the credit score.

❖ Credit utilization, or the way credit is used. Borrowers who borrow to the limit of their credit cards are considered higher risk.

❖ Having both a checking and savings account can improve your credit score.

❖ Credit history, or how long the borrower has been borrowing. Someone who has had credit for a long time is considered less risky.

❖ Inquiries into the applications for credit. The number of times a person has asked for credit or has had an inquiry into their credit record affects the credit score. Frequent requests for credit or frequent inquiries in a short period of time bring down the credit score.

❖ Types of credit in use—secured credit card, installment loans, revolving loans, or finance company lines.

Practicing more responsible borrowing and repayment habits will help improve your FICO score. One thing to be aware of is that while consolidating your bills and closing some of your credit cards may seem like a good idea at first in an attempt to raise your FICO score, it can actually negatively affect it. It brings you closer to your credit limit by removing available credit without reducing your existing debt.

As you can see, your credit score is determined by a number of factors and it is important to take all of these into consideration before taking any action. Improving your FICO score is not something that happens overnight, but taking steps now will get you far on the road to less debt and more cash.

Protecting Your Identity

The first step in protecting your credit history is protecting your identity. At the end of 1999, the Privacy Rights Clearinghouse reported that around 400,000 victims a year fall prey to someone stealing their identity, and that number is increasing by about 40 percent annually.

We tend to blame networked computers and the Internet for much of identity theft, but in fact, identity theft is really a low-tech crime. It is easy to lose your identity and it can take several years to regain it. Very often people don't even know that someone is using their name, Social Security number, or other identification until individuals who in normal circumstances are considered credit-worthy are turned down for a loan or a mortgage because someone using their identity has damaged their credit-worthiness. This is why it is imperative to check your credit report, at the very least biannually, even when you are not applying for credit.

Your identity can be easily stolen and it is up to you to take measures to protect it. There are many ways people can steal your identity. People can call the credit bureau posing as landlords, auto dealers, or mortgage lenders and obtain a complete copy of your credit report with all your account numbers printed on it.

If you leave "junk mail" lying around to deal with later, the preapproved offers for credit cards can easily be taken by someone who is in your home. The old proverb "One man's junk is another man's treasure" has more serious implications in this example that can lead to *your* credit-worthiness being destroyed. Someone can take the offer, fill it out with their address, use the credit card when it arrives, ignore the bills and ignore the calls from creditors. The bad credit goes on your credit report under your name. You can avoid this theft by giving more importance to these offers when they arrive in your mailbox and shredding them before you toss them into the wastebasket.

Act Quickly

If someone has stolen your identity, it is imperative that you act as soon as possible by notifying the authorities. Make sure that you keep a record of all documents, phone calls, and names of people you talk with to produce to the credit card companies, credit bureaus, or whomever might need it. You will also want to put a fraud alert on your credit report by writing or calling the credit bureaus to notify them of the situation. Fraud alerts usually remain on your credit report for two years. There are other actions you can take that are relatively common-sense depending on the type of fraud. Call your credit card company if your credit cards are stolen and notify the bank if your checks are stolen, and do it immediately.

Credit Solicitations

Stopping credit solicitations is a great way to protect your credit. Eliminating or greatly reducing the number of credit solicitations you receive in the mail will help in reducing your chance that someone will use one of these to perpetrate credit fraud on you.

In accordance with the provisions of the Fair Credit Reporting Act (FCRA) as amended in 1996, you have the right to tell the credit bureaus and other direct-mail marketing list brokers that you do not give permission for your name to be on their lists.

Since you don't need these pre-approved credit cards anymore, take your name off the marketing lists of four major credit bureaus by calling 1-888-5OPT-OUT (1-888-567-8688). You'll be glad you did. This is an automated system, so have your Social Security number, zip code, and telephone number ready to dial in. You will be asked to choose from the following options:

* ❖ Prevent solicitation for two years.
* ❖ Put your name back on the list after removing it.
* ❖ Permanently remove your name from the solicitation list.

If you want your name removed from the lists, you will receive a notification letter in the mail asking you to sign and confirm your intent. Although there may be other resources for mailing lists, this should cut credit offers dramatically.

While you're at it, if you would like to stay off other direct-mail marketing lists, write a letter giving your complete name, with any variations such as initials or middle names, and your mailing address to:

Mail Preference Service
Direct Marketing Association
PO Box 9008
Farmingdale, NY 11735

To remove your name from telephone solicitation lists, send your complete name, address, and phone number with area code to:

Telephone Preference Service
Direct Marketing Association
PO Box 9014
Farmingdale, NY 11735

Reviewing Your Credit Report

You should examine your credit report at least twice a year. In examining your report, it is important that you be on the lookout for any erroneous listings on your credit report. While it is necessary to question any irregularities and contact the credit bureau with any challenges, it is a federal offense to lie when disputing your credit report.

To get a copy of your credit report, contact the three major credit bureaus. If you have been denied credit within the past 60 days, they will issue a free report to you. If you live in Colorado, Georgia, Maryland, Massachusetts, New Jersey, or Vermont, you can get a report at no charge; otherwise, the charge is $8 unless your state has arranged a different fee with the credit bureaus. When I last checked, Maine's cost was $3 and Connecticut's was $5. All of the credit bureaus may not have the same information, so you will have to look at all three.

There are offers on the Internet to send you a compilation of all three. Only Experian and Equifax allow online delivery, so the three-agency report must be sent to you by mail; you may find several companies that make this offer for various prices.

To order the credit reports, you need to send them copies of some identification that shows your name and address. Your driver's license, a recent utility bill, or a recent credit card bill will do just fine. You also need to include your signature with the letter so they know you are authorizing the credit report. You may order your report and your spouse's at the same time, but your spouse must include the same information and also sign the letter. There are stiff fines and possible imprisonment for ordering a credit report without proper authorization.

Experian
National Consumer Assistance Center
PO Box 949
Allen, TX 75013-0949
1-888-397-3742
www.experian.com

Equifax
Information Service Center
PO Box 740241
Atlanta, GA 30374-0241
1-800-685-1111
www.equifax.com

Trans Union Corporation
Consumer Disclosure Center
PO Box 390
Springfield, PA 19064-0390
1-800-888-4213
www.transunion.com

If you have a spotty credit history, you may feel shy about asking for your credit reports. You can't clean them up if you don't know what is in them. Don't waste time beating yourself up; just boldly ask for your credit report and do what you need to do to fix it.

If you need some help creating a form to order your credit reports, try this as an example.

After you have received your credit reports, go over them very carefully and make sure that they are correct. If you find that you have old credit cards or store cards still on your credit report, call the creditors and ask them to close the accounts and inform the appropriate credit bureau. Each of the three major credit bureaus is supposed to inform the others of changes you requested, but you will need to look the next time you get your credit report to see if it was done.

While it would be ideal to have a perfect or near-perfect credit report, the reality is that many people have negative marks on their credit history and still get loans. This doesn't mean that you won't be able to get credit; it just might affect the size of the down payment required to make your purchase or the rate of interest.

Today's Date

Credit Reporting Agency Name
Address
City, State, Zip

Dear Madam or Sir:

I hereby request my credit report.

Your Name: _____

Your Home Telephone Number: _____

Your Social Security Number: _____

Date of Birth: _____

Current Address: _____

_____

_____

Lived here as of: _____

Previous Address: _____

_____

_____

Lived here as of: _____

Spouse's Name: _____

As proof of my identification and current residence, enclosed is a copy of (enclose a copy of one of the following: your driver's license, a recent bill, or a recent credit card bill).

Thank you very much for your kind attention to this.

Sincerely,

/Your Signature/

Your Name

An example of a credit report request letter.

Restoring Your Credit Rating When in Collections

If you are currently in collections (or ever are in collections in the future) it is important that you negotiate your credit rating with the lender and the collection agency before settling your debt. You can do this in a number of ways. Creditors and collection agencies care about getting their money, not about destroying your life. You can negotiate your credit rating listing with them in return for your payment. Do not get me wrong—it is not an option to not pay them. But it is possible for you to get the collection agency to agree to remove their listing and the creditor to list your credit rating after the settlement as "Paid as Agreed." You may not actually be able to get this ideal scenario, but you should be able to negotiate some better status than "Paid Collection," which is what you will receive with no negotiation.

Protecting Your Social Security Number

Don't carry your Social Security card, birth certificate, passport, or any credit cards you don't use in your wallet. Cancel the credit cards and put the other three documents in your safe deposit box.

Don't give your Social Security number to anyone except the IRS, your employer, and verifiable financial institutions. Your IRA account will be filed under your Social Security number. Don't use it as identification and don't give it out over the phone to anybody! If you are told that it will be used strictly to protect your identity, offer to use your birth date or some other series of numbers you will remember. Perhaps the last four digits on your Social Security number will suffice.

You may have to change your Social Security number if you have exhausted all efforts to regain your identity. This is a time-consuming and imperfect process and involves not only extensive paperwork in all aspects of your life, but ensuring that only correct and applicable credit history is transferred into your new file. This drastic measure should only be pursued when all efforts to regain your identity (meaning stopping the person who is using it) have been exhausted.

Protecting your identity and Social Security number will assist you in protecting yourself against fraud, but it will not stop it completely. We are always in danger of being damaged unknowingly by someone masquerading as us. This is why it is necessary to constantly check up on our credit report to make sure that there are no mistakes.

Protecting Your Cash from Disability

Women insure everything: house, cars, even their television set, but often we don't insure our ability to earn an income. The unforeseen effects of disability on our cash flow can ruin us financially if we don't take steps now while we are healthy.

Disability insurance is a necessary expenditure in protecting your cash. Many of us deal with the unpleasant thought of disability by not purchasing insurance. As too many unsuspecting people have learned, sticking our heads in the sand does not mean that disability won't happen. Disability insurance protects us in case illness or injury causes us to be unable to work.

According to the Senate Finance Committee report in 1999, 70 percent of applicants for Social Security Disability Insurance are denied benefits by the Social Security Administration. According to the Disability Management Sourcebook, the number of people with severe disabilities between the ages of 17 and 44 has increased 400 percent in 25 years.

There are two types of disability policies: group and individual. Group policies are purchased through your employer and are typically less expensive than individual policies. Individual disability policies are purchased on your own through an insurance agent. If your employer offers a group policy, you should sign up for it immediately and then decide if the coverage amount is adequate before determining if you will need to purchase an individual policy to supplement it. If your employer does not offer group disability, you will need to purchase an individual policy to cover all of your disability insurance. One word of caution on group policies is that they are typically not portable if you leave your employer.

Protecting Your Cash in Your Golden Years

There is a 50/50 chance you will have a major long-term-care expense in your lifetime, according to the *Employee Benefits Journal* (Vol. 21, No. 4). Because women typically live longer than their husbands, we must take decisive action now in determining how we are going to take care of ourselves when we are alone.

We all get old, and as people are living longer than ever, it is conceivable that we will spend just as much time in our retirement years as we spent in our working years. Long-term-care insurance is particularly important in protecting your cash later in life—especially for women. Long-term-care insurance is insurance that will cover your stay in a nursing home or assisted-living center. Nothing will deplete your savings faster than an extended stay in a nursing home.

If you are counting on Medicaid to pay for long-term care, think again. Medicaid will pay for it, but you nearly have to be broke to qualify. When planning for retirement, a long-term-care policy is a necessary component of a retirement plan.

Protecting Your Cash Through Times of Illness

Nothing can deplete your cash faster than an illness. Besides the effect it may have on your ability to work, if you are uninsured or underinsured, you will be faced with a mountain of medical bills.

Even though most of us have some sort of health insurance, there is still a large group of people for whom insurance is not affordable or is affordable only if they purchase plans with insufficient coverage. Only the very poor, with less than $716 in monthly income, can get help from Medicaid. According to the Kaiser Commission on Medicaid and the Uninsured, at www.kff.org, one in five women in the United States is uninsured. This amounts to 85.1 million American women between the ages of 18 and 64.

Even if we have the top-of-the-line insurance offered to us and we can afford the premiums, what the medical facility charges us for our care and what the insurance company feels is "reasonable and customary" are often not close enough for our pocketbooks. Don't take this lying down. Get out your negotiating hat and see what you can do. But don't deny yourself the medical care you need.

I had a comprehensive insurance policy when I was diagnosed with breast cancer. Since I lived in Scottsdale, Arizona, I went to the Mayo clinic near my home, which has a good reputation for working with cancer patients. I showed my insurance card and scheduled the surgery. While I was healing from the surgery, I had appointments with a chemotherapy oncologist and a radiation oncologist about the next steps to take. I had some choices, and when I talked to my surgeon, she told me about the nature of my tumor and said that radiation was really necessary. Although chemotherapy was an optional treatment, she showed me the statistics and gave her professional opinion that I would decrease my chances of that kind of cancer returning by 12 to 15 percent. That was good enough for me.

Before the treatments started, I had an appointment with the patient accounts department. I was told that they had reviewed the cost of my treatments with my insurance company and that my out-of-pocket costs would be somewhere between $30,000 and $50,000 depending on complications. There was no hurry to make my decision.

I reviewed my net worth statement and decided that I had enough borrowing power so that without cashing in my tax-deferred retirement accounts, I could pay that bill if I could work out a long-term payment plan. I went back to the patient accounts woman and asked about the finance charges and what kind of payment plan we could work out.

She asked for my net worth statement and called me later. She said that Mayo didn't want anyone to lose their house or be under undue stress over the money when the treatments are going on, and that after they were over we would set up a payment plan and there would be no interest charged.

By the time I was finished with the treatments, I had a bill for $71,000. Was I worth it? You bet! The insurance company, which was in Pennsylvania, had paid me $17,000 because that was "reasonable and customary" for the area I lived in. I asked how long ago that allowance was set, because my area in Arizona has boomed in the last few years. My customer support representative said she would look into it, and a few weeks later she called me back to tell me that I was right, they needed to upgrade their decision and they were sending me some more money.

When I made the appointment to set up my payment plan, I was down to $21,000 out-of-pocket and the Mayo clinic gave me a good-faith discount so that my new bill was $17,000. This is certainly not a secured debt and I was surprised that they didn't give me a contract on our payment agreement, but I will keep my promise. After all, I'm here to do it.

Money Therapy

Olivia Mellan

You always have the power to negotiate. It's your money. Make sure you come up with a payment plan that works for you—even with hospitals and the IRS. You always have a choice. Make choices that take care of your financial matters and that support you as well. Don't let anybody take your choices away.

Protecting What You Own

Besides having enough insurance to take care of losses to your home, your car, and your personal property, you need to protect your money.

Many folks feel that they don't have to do any estate planning because they don't have a large estate. But all of us do need to have some legal documents in place. If you own anything at all and you care what happens to it after you die, you need to make provisions for it.

Property can be transferred in three ways:

- ❖ By title
- ❖ By contract
- ❖ By will

Each will be described in the sections that follow.

By Title

Assets held *jointly with rights of survivorship* (JTWROS) will be passed on to the other owner at the death of one of them. This supercedes your will. Your half of the assets is added to the value of your estate and goes to the surviving co-owner. You can sell your half of the property without the consent of the other owner, but the assets will transfer to that person if you die.

The *tenancy in common* title covers property owned by several people, and your will dictates where your share will go at your death. Like with the JTWROS, you can sell your share while you are living.

Tenancy by the entirety is only between spouses and is not available in all states. Property that is titled this way is transferred outside the will to the surviving spouse, and unlike JTWROS or property owned through tenancy in common, tenancy by the entirety can be severed only with the consent of both spouses. In other words, a husband can't sell his half of the property without his wife's consent, which is often an issue in divorce or separation.

By Contract

A second way to transfer property is by contract. This type of transfer depends on how the beneficiaries are designated on the contract. Insurance policies, trusts, IRAs, annuities, and retirement plans such as 401(k) and 403(b) are examples of property transferred by contract.

If you change beneficiaries, be sure that the documents are amended to reflect your change. In working with clients, I have found this area is often overlooked. One elderly woman's insurance was left to her mother who had been dead for years. Single men who made their parents their beneficiaries and forgot to change the policy when they married ... well, need I say more? Ex-spouses sometimes leave their money to the other parent of their children, assuming that she will distribute it to them later. You don't want to assume anything that you really want to happen. Take care of it yourself.

By Will

The third and most common way to leave property at death is through a will. Even if you think you don't have much of value, stating where you want your things to go will make life easier for your family and friends. That way there is no mistake about your intentions. Wills can be handwritten holographic wills, or they can be quite involved. I suggest that any will be blessed by an attorney to make sure that it does what you want it to do and that it complies with the laws of the state where you live.

I've heard lots of reasons why people refuse to get around to making a will:

> "I'm too young to worry about dying."
>
> "I don't have much to leave anybody."
>
> "I just haven't had time."
>
> "My husband and I have everything owned jointly, so if I die it will all be his anyway."

This last one is especially detrimental to couples with children from former marriages. I always ask, "Do you really think that your husband's grown children will give your grown kids their share after he dies, especially if he didn't have a will either?"

Money opens all kinds of doors to greed.

Besides your will, you should leave a *Letter of Instruction*. This is not a legal document, but information to your family or friends about funeral arrangements or where you want to be buried or have your ashes strewn. This is also the place where you can leave your engagement ring to your oldest daughter so that it is clear that's what you intended at the end of your life, no matter how many people you promised it to over the years.

If you die without a will, you will have died intestate and the state will decide where your possessions and any money that is not titled or in a contract with up-to-date beneficiaries will go. The state may also decide who will raise your children, so be sure that you have made provisions for a legal guardian in your will. Don't let that be a surprise to anyone! Get their consent before you name them. Generally, legal guardians are appointed for children under 18 or 21, but you can determine an older age in your will. Even if you are married, it is a good thing for each of you to make this provision in case you and your partner are killed in a common accident.

Your executor will be your personal representative after you die. This may be a relative or friend or a professional organization such as a bank or trust company that specializes in estate and trust management. It is your choice. This is a big responsibility, and whoever fulfills this role should be compensated, which can also be part of the terms of your will.

Although each of the 41 common-law states may have some different laws governing the transferring of property at death, there are 9 community-property states, which are also unique from each other: Arizona, California, Idaho, Louisiana, Nevada, New Mexico, Texas, Washington, and Wisconsin. That is why estate attorneys need to be involved.

Get Your Docs in a Row

In protecting your cash, it is necessary to spell out your wishes regarding your property and your health if you are incapacitated. Three other documents that everyone over 18 should have whether they are married or single and whether they own any property or not are …

❖ A living will.

❖ A durable power of attorney for healthcare.

❖ A durable power of attorney for property.

A living will is a document that tells everyone what your wishes are regarding life support at the end of your life. This must be very specific and include not only resuscitation but also nourishment given through feeding tubes, which will just keep you alive. Most hospitals require that their patients have a living will on file and your doctors and family members need to know about your wishes. In some states, these expire and need to be renewed. Check with your doctor or medical facility.

A durable power of attorney for healthcare is a legal document naming the person who can speak for you with regard to health or medical issues if you can't speak for yourself. This is in addition to the living will. The person holding this power must know you very well and you need to discuss with them while you can, how you would like them to represent you. It is also important for spouses to have these documents even if they name each other.

A durable power of attorney for property is a legal document that gives the holder a tremendous amount of power and responsibility. This person can act in your behalf on any property you own. Besides writing checks and paying bills, this might include selling or transferring property, changing beneficiaries on trusts, insurance, and other contracts. Again, this person needs to know you well and act as you would act if you could do it yourself. If you have property in your own name, your spouse would have to have this legal power to act in your behalf.

The word *durable* is important in these titles because you can give "special power of attorney" to someone like a real estate agent so that papers can be signed in your absence, but the power is gone when the single transaction is completed.

The durable power of attorney for healthcare and the durable power of attorney for property end the moment you die and the executor or administrator appointed by your will, or by the court if you die intestate, takes over to administer the business of your estate. These durable powers are given through legal documents drawn up by an attorney according to the laws of the state in which you have your legal residence. If you move to another state, be sure that they are in compliance with that state's laws.

Coaching Tip

Software applications like Family Lawyer (from The Learning Company, Inc.®) provides you all these legal documents and lets you tailor them to your own use. You can add your personal information and print them out ready to be signed.

Give Some Money Away

There are many opportunities to give our money away. Just as we made a plan to pay off our debts and set goals, which we funded in special accounts, it is important to determine where we will give our money and stick to the plan. That is not to say that we may not choose a different charity each year, but similar to buying stocks in companies we like and want to support, we support organizations and individuals by charitable donations. Watching our net worth grow bigger and bigger is a lot more fun when we realize that we have enough to share.

You will take deductions for the money you give to legitimate charitable or nonprofit organizations. If you question their status, call the local Better Business Bureau and check them out. Don't make a contribution over the phone with your credit card unless you have made the call and you are sure that you have the right number. The Public Broadcasting System (PBS) is one of my favorite charities and I like to renew my membership when they are having a fund drive and someone has offered to match donations for a period of time. There is nothing I can do but give my credit card number, but I always make a note of the call and check my next statement for validity.

As I mentioned earlier, any individual can give any other individual $10,000 each year without incurring a tax consequence to either party. That means that a couple could give a child and her spouse $40,000 altogether. You can give as much as you want to pay someone's medical bills or tuition for education as long as the payment is made directly to a qualified institution. Be sure to verify that the organization is qualified by the IRS before you write the check.

Remember Grandpa's mantra, "Money is to be used and shared, but not wasted."

The Bottom Line

You are the guardian of your assets and credit. It is up to you to secure yourself against loss as much as possible. Become your own watchdog.

Reader's Journal:

Knowledge Gained:

_____

_____

_____

_____

_____

_____

_____

_____

_____

_____

Steps I Will Take:

_____

_____

_____

_____

_____

_____

_____

_____

_____

_____

This book is full of stories about women like you and me. I'd like to conclude the book with the most important story of all—your story. Please take the time to think about how you would complete the following story:

_____ (your name) is a _____-year-old woman who has chosen to upgrade her financial life so that she can _____. In fact, the obstacle to less debt, more cash she most wants to overcome is _____. She plans to do it by _____. Her lifetime relationship with money could be described as _____. Her strongest money influence was her _____, who believed _____. As a result, she carries with her a set of money voices that say _____. If you were to ask her to name her most satisfying money experience, she would tell you it was _____. Today, as an adult, her greatest financial strength is _____, and it has served her by _____. In terms of money personality, _____ (your name) could be considered a _____, meaning she _____. She counteracts this natural tendency by _____. When it comes to organizing money, she prefers to _____. Her organizing tools of choice include _____. When she looks back on her financial life, she wants to be able to know that _____. In fact, in order to be able to say this, she took some intentional steps to reduce her debt and increase her cash. Those steps included _____. She is grateful for the money she has, and is eager to earn more so that she can _____.

When it comes to giving to others, _____ (your name) enjoys contributing to _____

She is enthused about the future she is creating, and is especially excited about her plans to _____. The money message she would most like to give to the people she cares about is that _____. _____ (your name) enjoyed the saying, "If your horse is dead, get off it," and realized the dead horse she needed to get off in terms of what wasn't working for her financially was _____. She did get off it and became a woman of financial strength who worked her plan and enjoyed a life of less debt and more cash.

Chapter 13

Getting to Where You Want to Be

The Bottom Line

The real story here is not your money, it is you. You are the one who will inhabit your future, and you are the one who can make it the future you want to live.

Now, read your story as if it were someone else's. This will give you a chance to step away from your situation and see it more clearly, with less emotion. The value of looking at your money life objectively is that it enables you to separate your money from your identity. You are not your money, and your money is not you. Your debt is just a number and so is your net worth. Numbers can be re-arranged with simple choices.

What You Still Want to Know

You've digested a lot of information, but no book can tell you everything you want to know. What else do you want to know about less debt and more cash?

_____

_____

_____

_____

_____

How will you find out what you want to know? Look it up in other books, ask a knowledgeable friend, meet with a financial advisor, or browse financial sites on the Internet.

Money Therapy

There is something very therapeutic about taking things one step at a time. Each step seems to produce energy for the next. Be sure to build in rewards for your effort, although you will find the satisfaction of working your plan, item by item, is often reward enough.

Olivia Mellan

Moving Forward

What have you done and what needs to be done? Place a check mark by those things you have already done or are doing.

- ❏ Organize my money life to fit my personal style
- ❏ Identify the torpedoes that could sabotage my effort
- ❏ Build in triggers to keep me motivated
- ❏ Identify my money personality
- ❏ Identify my money patterns
- ❏ Identify my money beliefs
- ❏ Identify my money voices
- ❏ Examine my money history

- ☐ Select new patterns and beliefs I want to establish
- ☐ Name where I am financially
- ☐ Name where I want to be financially
- ☐ Understand the rules of the debt game
- ☐ Look at my credit report
- ☐ Correct errors on my credit report
- ☐ Identify the order of debt I will pay off
- ☐ Notify creditors of my plan to pay them
- ☐ Return any credit cards I do not use
- ☐ Ask to be removed from direct mail lists
- ☐ Contact credit counseling services for help
- ☐ Talk about money with my partner or spouse
- ☐ Talk about money with the children in my life
- ☐ Talk about money with my parents
- ☐ Get all of my financial information in one place
- ☐ Open my bills as they come
- ☐ Place my bills in one place until time to pay them
- ☐ Assign a time and place to pay bills
- ☐ Purchase financial tools and software I feel are essential
- ☐ Find a financial Web site I enjoy and use
- ☐ Identify three ways to immediately spend smarter
- ☐ Order automatic withdrawal from my paycheck to a savings account or fund
- ☐ Order automatic withdrawal from my paycheck to a retirement or investment account
- ☐ Contribute to my company's retirement plan
- ☐ Contribute the most possible to my company's retirement plan
- ☐ Learn the computer
- ☐ Read about money every day
- ☐ Select my method of increasing my cash
- ☐ Ask for a raise
- ☐ Choose a second job
- ☐ Change jobs

❏ Start my own business

❏ Select the insurances I need

❏ Explore insurance policies and companies

❏ Buy the insurance I need

❏ Complete my cash flow statement

❏ Complete my net worth statement

❏ Create my monthly money plan, or budget

❏ Take steps to protect my credit and financial identity

❏ Interview at least two financial advisors

❏ Ask others who they use as advisors

❏ Write out what I want my life to be

❏ Set a timeline to achieve the life I want

❏ Other: _____

As you continue working your plan, check off the items when you complete them. You may want to enter your immediate plans in the following list:

1. Name your most urgent money task.

   _____

   How will you complete it? _____

   _____

2. Name your second most urgent money task.

   _____

   How will you complete it? _____

   _____

3. Name your third most urgent money task.

   _____

   How will you complete it? _____

   _____

Once you have completed these three tasks, repeat the process with another set of three tasks.

You Are Here

If someone asked you where you are in your money life, how would you describe your location on the path to less debt, more cash?

We began this book at the spot marked "You Are Here." Now you are in a different place. You have moved from where you were to where you are now, and the two places are very different from one another.

Anytime you learn something new, you have accelerated the travel time to your next destination. You have learned a lot about reducing your debt and increasing your cash. You have advanced your position on your path, and I am enthused about what that can do for your life.

Work Your Plan

Remember: Work your plan or your plan won't work.

Whether you have written it down or not, you probably have a short-term and long-term plan in mind. I strongly urge you to write it down so you can know if you're getting where you want to be.

Once you write out your plan, stick to it as if you'd be punished if you didn't. I had a client, Ruth, who religiously followed the plan we created for her. She said to me, "I'd like to go to my nephew's graduation. He is the valedictorian, but the airfare isn't on my budget so I guess I can't go." I asked her how many times in life will the nephew you love be valedictorian at his high school graduation? She veered from her budget to purchase the tickets, and she did the right thing. There are times to flex your plan, but do it rarely and only for something as important as Ruth's trip.

Coaching Tip

When I started my business, my cash flow decreased for a time. To protect my financial situation, I chose to cut out costly activities like eating at restaurants. This was an adjustment for my friends who were used to me joining them frequently for dinner. I simply said, "That's not how I'm spending my money right now." We got together in other ways that didn't put me at risk. I had a plan and I stuck to it. Because of that, I can once again enjoy fine dining. My advice to you is make your choices and stick to them. It's worth it.

Keep Learning

I hope to see you at an Everywoman's Money Conference or at one of the many other Everywoman's Money events. There are many other events and activities in your area that will increase your knowledge about money and keep you resolved to become more and more money smart.

Keep reading, keep talking, keep saving and investing, keep learning. Knowledge gives you the power to know what to do.

Take a Vow

Vow to keep your promise to yourself. Read the following intentions. Select one at a time to repeat to yourself as you move through your days. These intentions are read as a group by the women at the Everywoman's Money Conferences. Imagine yourself reading this aloud with over a thousand other women. Hear your voice join theirs:

❖ I will give up self-limiting beliefs about money.

❖ I will start today, right where I am.

❖ I will stay with what works for me and give up what doesn't.

❖ I will learn the language of money.

❖ I will only buy things I really want.

❖ I will talk freely about money.

❖ I will make a habit of investing.

❖ I will manage my money on paper and not in my head.

❖ I will give up the need for instant gratification.

❖ I will give myself time to create the life I want.

❖ I will take action. Now.

©The Everywoman's Company

Where's Alice Everywoman?

In Lewis Carroll's book *Alice's Adventure in Wonderland*, Alice meets the Cheshire Cat:

> Alice asks, "Would you tell me, please, which way I ought to go from here?"

"That depends a good deal on where you want to get to," says the Cat.

"I don't much care where," says Alice.

"Then it doesn't matter which way you go," says the Cat.

"So long as I get somewhere," Alice adds.

"Oh, you're sure to do that," says the Cat, "if you only walk long enough."

Cheshire Cat was right. Walk long enough in any direction and you will get somewhere. Trouble is, somewhere is often a place you wouldn't choose to be. As long as you're walking, walk toward the life you want.

It has been a pleasure to help you move forward on your financial path, and I wish you great success as a money-smart woman.

The Bottom Line

Only you can do it, and you *can* do it!

Reader's Journal:

Knowledge Gained:

_____

_____

_____

_____

_____

_____

_____

_____

_____

Steps I Will Take:

_____

_____

_____

_____

_____

_____

_____

_____

_____

Glossary

accrue To increase. When interest accrues on your loan, it accumulates according to the current interest rate for that loan and the amount you owe.

adjusted balance method The best approach to calculating the monthly finance charge on a credit card from the point of view of the consumer. The finance charge is based on the amount you owe, after all payments are applied to your balance.

adjustable rate mortgages (ARMs) A mortgage for a fixed amount of debt, for a fixed period of time, with a variable rate of interest. ARMs typically have a maximum annual increase limit of 2 percent and an overall cap on total interest rate increase of 6 percent.

amortization To put money aside on a regular basis, typically a sinking fund for the gradual repayment of debt. Also, to write off expenditures for tax purposes over a fixed period of time.

annual percentage rate (APR) In terms of mortgages, the APR includes all points paid and interest paid over the life of the loan. For variable rate mortgages, this rate will change as the interest rate changes.

ARMs *See* adjustable rate mortgages.

assets Any possession that has value upon exchange.

ATM (automatic teller machine) An electronic device that allows you to withdraw money from a number of personal accounts such as checking accounts, savings accounts, and credit card accounts. They frequently charge a minimum transaction fee of $1 to $2 that is automatically deducted from your account.

auto insurance A property and casualty insurance policy that provides protection from the risks of loss that would result from a car accident. Coverage typically includes protection for liability damages incurred as a result of striking another car or property that results in property damage and/or injury to others. In addition, coverage is provided for physical property loss due to collision, fire, theft, or other physical damages to the owned vehicle. Other coverage can include medical payments for nonrelated persons traveling in the insured vehicle, towing expense, and rental reimbursement.

average daily balance Outstanding daily balance of a line of credit, divided by the number of days in the billing period.

average daily balance method The next best and most commonly used approach to calculating the monthly finance charge on a credit card from the consumer's point of view. Interest is charged based on the "average daily balance" of the account over the course of the billing period.

award letter Once a student has been admitted to a school and has completed the financial aid process, she will receive an offer of financial assistance, often called an award letter. Each school that accepts you will send you its own award letter that tells you what you are eligible to receive at that school for the year.

balance sheet A financial statement that provides a snapshot of a person's or business' financial position. A listing of net worth: assets and liabilities as of a specific date.

balloon mortgages A mortgage with a fixed amount of debt and a fixed or variable rate of interest. Typically, payment is made for a fixed period of time, after which the entire loan comes due.

bridge loan A short-term loan, usually six months to one year in term, designed to provide funds for a short period of time, payable in full at the end of the period. Usually incurred in anticipation of a future event, such as the sale of a home or other asset, or the anticipated receipt of future income.

capitalize To add unpaid accrued interest to unpaid principal. This increases your total outstanding principal. Thus, if you choose a lender that capitalizes once a year or more, you may be paying interest on interest.

cash advance A withdrawal of cash from a credit card, usually from an ATM, which results in an unsecured debt. Many cards charge a minimum fee at the time the advance is made in addition to charging interest from the date of the advance.

cash flow statement A financial statement that provides detailed information about income and expenses over a period of time.

cash value insurance A life insurance contract that builds cash value over a period of years.

certificate of deposit (CD) A debt instrument typically issued by a bank that pays a fixed rate of interest for a known period of time. Maturities range from several weeks to several years.

coinsurance The sharing of a potential risk between the insured and the insurance company. A common feature of health insurance policies, this provision requires that the insured pay a percentage of the loss up to the maximum "stop loss limit" following the payment of a deductible. *See also* stop loss provision.

collateral An asset that is pledged as security against the default of a loan.

compound interest Interest that is paid or received on interest from prior periods. *See also* simple interest.

capitalize As used in reference to investing: to use or convert to capital; to establish the stock of a new business at a certain price; to supply capital to a business; to use something to one's advantage.

consolidation A method of combining several loans into a single loan with an extended repayment term of up to 30 years. This can be an effective method of lowering your monthly payment.

consumer debt Nonmortgage debt that is used to fund consumer-related purchases; common examples include auto loans and revolving debt used to purchase other personal use goods.

co-sign   To take on the responsibility for debt repayment along with the person assuming the primary responsibility for loan repayment. In the event of default on the loan by the primary debtor, full responsibility for repayment of the debt falls to the co-signer.

credit card   A piece of plastic with which one can incur unsecured consumer debt.

credit collection agency   A business involved in the collection of debt for a third party.

credit limit   Maximum available credit on a given line of credit or credit card.

credit score   Rating of an individual's creditworthiness as defined by a formula. Used by lenders to evaluate the risk involved in extending credit or offering a loan to an individual or business.

current assets   Readily accessible assets that are held as cash or can be easily converted to cash. Liquid assets such as cash, or money held in a checking or savings account or money market fund or account.

current liabilities   Debts that are due within a short period of time, typically one to six months.

dead beat   A person who avoids the payment of debt.

debit card   The electronic equivalent of a check, which automatically withdraws money (debits) from your checking or savings account.

debt   An obligation or liability.

debtor   A person who incurs a liability or debt; the one who is obligated to repay a debt.

deductible   The amount the insured must pay in the event of a loss before coverage is provided by the policy. The deductible amount is always stated in the policy.

default   Failure to repay a loan. Although loans can vary dramatically, you are typically considered in default if you have made no payments for 180 days and are not in your grace period, deferment, or forbearance. This will negatively affect your credit rating for many years.

deferment   A time when you are not required to make payments. During the deferment, interest continues to accrue on the loan. Deferments may be granted for reasons such as half-time study, unemployment, economic hardship, graduate fellowships, and rehabilitation training.

deficit spending   Spending that exceeds income over a given period of time.

delinquency   Failure to make a loan payment when it is due. If you are more than 90 days delinquent, your delinquency will be reported to the national credit bureaus and will negatively affect your credit rating. If you are delinquent for 180 days or more, you are considered in default.

disbursement   The date a loan check is issued by the lender. Some lenders issue loan funds electronically.

down payment   The initial deposit required when financing a purchase; the amount "put down" at time of purchase; a portion of the full purchase price. The size of the down payment can affect the number of "points" charged and/or the interest rate charged on a loan.

elimination period A disability insurance contract provision that stipulates the period of time between the onset of a covered disability and the date that the payment of benefits begin under the terms of the policy. See also "Waiting Period."

expected family contribution This is the amount that the federal government has determined that a student and family should be able to contribute toward the cost of education, including living expenses, for one year. The Expected Family Contribution is calculated by a standard formula, applied to all financial aid applicants nationally, that takes into consideration all of the information included on the FAFSA. The Expected Family Contribution is the same for all schools—without regard to the cost of the school. *See also* Free Application for Federal Student Aid (FAFSA).

Federal Housing Administration (FHA) FHA loans are available to qualifying individuals and families and carry slightly lower interest rates than are commercially available—with lower requirements for downpayments as well. FHA charges you an upfront premium for 30 years worth of FHA mortgage insurance, part of which will be returned to the buyer who pays the loan in full over the life of the loan.

first mortgage The primary debt position against real property.

fixed-rate mortgage A loan collateralized by real property—for a fixed

amount of debt, for a fixed period of time, at a fixed rate of interest, with a fixed payment.

forbearance Temporary end to or reduction of loan payments which may be granted in cases of financial difficulty when you are not eligible for a deferment. Interest continues to accrue on your account. Most commonly involves student loans.

foreclosure To call for the full payment of debt prior to full term of the loan—usually due to default of loan payments past due.

Free Application for Federal Student Aid (FASFA) The mandatory application required in order for a student to receive consideration for virtually all forms of financial aid. To determine a student's level of financial need, the U.S. Department of Education uses a standard formula, established by Congress, to evaluate the information included on the Free Application for Federal Student Aid (FAFSA). On the basis of this formula, the Expected Family Contribution (EFC) and Student Contribution levels are established.

future value The anticipated value of a present amount or stream of payments, assuming a given rate of inflation and return on investment, over a given period of time.

grace period For credit cards: a period of time during which no interest is payable—only if the balance is paid in full on or before the due date of the prior statement period. If the balance is not paid in full on or before the due date of the payment, interest is charged from the original date of purchase, with no grace period. Cash advances have no grace period. For insurance policies: a contract provision that requires a period of "grace" during which insurance remains in force without premium payment, in anticipation of payment. This contract provision prevents policy cancellation for a period of time, as defined in the policy contract, beyond the "premium due date."

graduated payment mortgages (GPMs)　A mortgage with a fixed amount of debt for a fixed period of years, with a fixed or variable interest rate, with a payment that starts low and gradually increases over the life of the loan. In the early years, the payment is usually not enough to cover interest charges, resulting in increased debt and increased total interest charges over the life of the loan.

guaranteed renewable　A term usually used in reference to a health insurance, disability insurance, or long-term care insurance policy. This contract provision states that the policy cannot be cancelled as long as premiums are paid in a timely manner. Premiums are not guaranteed to remain unchanged, however. If premiums are raised, the increase must apply to an entire group as opposed to individual selection. (Example: a 15 percent rate increase for all females is possible. A 15 percent rate increase for an individual is not possible.)

guaranty agency　The organization that insures Federal Stafford and PLUS, GNMA, VA, or FHA loans for lenders. If you default on a loan, the guaranty agency will pay the lender and will then collect the loan directly from you.

home equity line of credit (HELOC)　A flexible line of credit against the accumulated equity of a residence, typically a second mortgage, with a variable interest rate charged on the outstanding credit balance only. Interest is generally charged on the average daily balance. Minimum payment due is sometimes interest only, or interest plus 1 to 2 percent of the outstanding balance. Payments in excess of the required minimum can (and should) be made at any time without pre-payment penalty.

home equity (HE) loan　A fixed loan against the accumulated equity of a residence, typically a second mortgage, usually for a fixed period of time (typically 1 to 10 years) at a fixed rate of interest with a fixed monthly payment. HE loans can also be variable rate loans. *See also* home equity line of credit (HELOC).

homeowner's insurance　A contract of insurance that protects the named insured from loss as the result of physical damage to a principal residence. Liability protection is also frequently provided which protects the homeowner and dependents from claims for personal injury caused by the named insured(s). Not all Homeowner's insurance policies are alike in terms of covered perils or limits. The HO-3 contract offers the most comprehensive coverage against a wide assortment of perils but does not cover property damage caused by flood or earthquake. Be sure to understand what your homeowners policy does and does not cover.

insured　The individual or business that is protected from risk of loss by a contract of insurance.

interest Usually stated as a percentage or dollar amount. For debt: money you must pay for the "privilege" of borrowing money, expressed as a percentage of the outstanding principal. For fixed income investments: the yield or return on an investment. Income received as a result of lending money.

investment assets Assets that are held by an individual or business with an expectation of return of income or growth of principal. Not a personal use asset.

landlord's insurance Property and casualty insurance that provides protection to a landlord in the event of property or casualty loss.

late payment fee A charge that is levied for late payment of a minimum balance due on a line of credit or credit card. This charge is added to the prior balance due. Late payment will also generally trigger the loss of any low introductory interest rate offered by a credit card company and can affect a person's credit history and credit score.

lessor The owner of a leased asset who receives income for allowing another party use of the asset.

lessee The user of a leased asset that pays the lessor for the right to use the asset.

liability An obligation to pay, a responsibility.

liability insurance Commercial insurance that provides for protection against the potential financial loss for the insured in the event the insured was found responsible for injury or damages to another party.

line of credit An agreement by a lender to loan money to a customer, on an "as needed" basis, up to a certain amount at a pre-determined rate of interest.

loan A debt issue, typically due within 1 to 10 years.

maturity date The date on which a financial contract becomes due, as in the case of a loan, CD, or bond instrument.

minimum payment The minimum amount due on an outstanding balance of a loan, typically represents interest charges for the period plus 1 to 2 percent of the outstanding balance.

minimum payment due The absolute minimum that must be paid on a line of credit or credit card to avoid default.

mortgage Debt using real property as collateral, typically for a fixed period of time, for a fixed or variable rate of interest. The pledging of real property to a creditor against the potential default of a loan.

mortgagee The debtor. The individual or entity assuming a liability that is collateralized by real property.

mortgage point *See* point.

mortgage lender The mortgagor. The person or entity offering the loan to the mortgagee, with real property held as collateral.

net worth statement A measure of value. Total assets minus total liabilities = net worth.

out-of pocket cost Maximum cost that can be incurred by the insured in the event of a loss. *See also* stop loss provision.

over-insured   To have insurance protection in excess of the potential value of loss as the result of a covered risk.

past due balance   Indicates that a prior payment has not been made before the payment due date. Past due balances must be paid in full to avoid possible foreclosure of the debt.

Pell Grant   The Federal Pell Grant is a needs-based grant for undergraduate students. It is the first level of funding of the financial aid package; other federal and private aid is added to it. Because the Pell Grant is a grant, it does not need to be paid back. The maximum award for the 1999 to 2000 award year is $3,125. The Pell Grant is awarded to all eligible students, but the amounts for future awards will depend on program funding.

Perkins Loan   The Federal Perkins Loan is a low-interest (5 percent) loan available to both undergraduate and graduate students who have exceptional financial need. This need is determined by a federal formula using the information provided on the Free Application for Federal Student Aid (FAFSA). The loan is made with government funds, but the school is the lender. Depending on when you apply, your level of need, and the school's funding level, this loan has the following limits. Undergraduates: $3,000 per year, $15,000 for the entire enrollment period; Graduate students: $5,000 per year, $30,000 for the entire enrolled period (including Federal Perkins Loans borrowed as an undergraduate).

permanent insurance   Life insurance that is intended to cover the risk of loss of life for the insured's full life.

personal use assets   Assets owned by an individual for their personal use or enjoyment.

point   A standard unit of value. For debt: typically, 1 percent of the loan amount. Points are considered "prepaid interest" and as such are income tax deductible. Points paid on the principal mortgage are deductible the year paid; points paid upon refinance are deductible over the life of the loan. For investing: typically a unit value of $1.00 used for quoting changes in stock prices. A bond point is equal to $10 (1 percent of $1000 face value).

pre-existing condition   A condition that existed prior to the issuance of insurance.

premium   Price. As used in insurance: the cost of insurance coverage for a stipulated period of time. As used in investments: trading at a price in excess of par.

present value   The current value of a future amount, or stream of payments, assuming a given rate of inflation and return on investment over a given period of time.

previous balance method   The worst method for determining the finance charge on a credit card from the point of view of the consumer. Interest is charged on the previous statement balance, as if no payments were made during the billing period.

principal   The full amount borrowed, or the balance of the loan that has not yet been repaid. This may include capitalized interest. Interest is calculated as a percentage of this amount.

promissory note   A contract with the lender that you, the borrower, sign before the loan is disbursed. This contract states that you will repay the loan and legally binds you to its terms and conditions.

real property An asset that consists of land and/or buildings.

refinance To restructure a debt or mortgage, typically to take advantage of reduced interest rates, to reduce payments, or to consolidate debt into one line of credit.

repayment schedule In reference to student loans, a document received shortly after leaving school that states the loan principal, the monthly payment amount, and provides a schedule of dates when payments are due.

revolving credit A legal commitment by a bank or other lending institution to loan money to a customer as needed up to a stated maximum limit, for a stipulated period of time which may extend for a number of years.

second mortgage A secondary debt position against real property.

secondary market In lending: a company that buys loans from lenders. Lenders often sell loans to secondary markets so that they can continually replenish their lending funds, which in turn get marketed to fixed income investors. In investing: the purchase or sale of an investment that takes place after the primary offering.

secured credit card A consumer credit card that is secured by deposits in a bank or other financial institution.

secured debt Debt that is secured by collateral.

self-insured An individual or business with sufficient assets to meet a potential financial loss from a known risk.

simple interest When interest is calculated using a "simple method," interest is calculated at the end of the period. To calculate the interest earned on $1000 earning 6 percent in a year, simply multiply $1000 by .06. The result is $60 interest earnings per year of "simple interest." *See also* compound interest.

stop loss provision An insurance term that defines the maximum loss potential of the insured. For example, a health insurance stop loss provision limits the maximum annual out-of-pocket cost to the insured to $1500 (the stated annual deductible of $500 plus $1000 or 20 percent of the co-insurance limit of $5000).

Student Aid Report (SAR) Received a couple of weeks after the Free Application for Federal Student Aid (FAFSA) is mailed to the processor. The SAR contains all the information provided on the FAFSA, messages from the processor, and some calculations. Upon receipt, the SAR should be reviewed to make sure that all of the information is correct.

Student Loan Marketing Association A nonprofit organization that buys student loans from many lenders and packages the loans to students, in an effort to help students consolidate their student loans into a more affordable, single loan. Sells packaged student loan portfolios to investors as a fixed-income security. Also known as "Sallie Mae."

subordinated debt   Debt that is in a lesser position in terms of security of principal. In the event of bankruptcy or liquidation, subordinated debt holders are paid after secured debtors. For example, a second mortgage is subordinate to the principal mortgage on a home.

subsidized loans   A loan that is supported by the lender or third party such as the Veterans Administration (VA) or the Small Business Administration (SBA). (For example, the Stafford student loan is a subsidized loan. The U.S. government pays the interest on this loan for you while you are in school, during your six-month grace period, and during periods of authorized deferment.)

Supplemental Educational Opportunity Grants (SEOG)   Available to undergraduates with exceptional financial need—those who have the lowest Expected Family Contribution. Students who receive Federal Pell Grants are given priority. Like all other grants, the SEOG does not need to be repaid. *See also* Pell Grant.

surrender charge   Also known as a "Contingent Deferred Charge" (CDSC). Typically, this is a reducing charge over a limited period of years. The charge imposed by the insurance company upon termination or surrender of a life insurance contract or annuity. The sales charge imposed upon the surrender of "B" or "C" shares of mutual funds.

surrender value   The amount payable in cash value available to the policy owner upon voluntarytermination of a cash value life insurance contract.

Policy surrender value equals cash value less surrender charges, if any, imposed by the contracts.

T-bill   A type of simple interest U.S. government security that matures (comes due) in one year or less. Available maturities are 13-week, 26-week, or 52-weeks. Interest payments on many debt instruments are tied to the T-bill rate. The investors who buy them are making a short-term loan to the federal government. (For example, the 52-week T-Bill matures in one year, meaning that the investor gets all of the original investment, plus interest, one year following the original investment date.) Issued in denominations of $10,000 to $1,000,000—in $5,000 increments.

tenant's insurance   Property and liability insurance that protects a person who leases property from another.

term   The length of time you have to repay a loan.

term insurance   Life insurance issued for a specified period of time for a specified annual premium. Term insurance does not typically have cash value.

time value of money   The value of money stated in terms of present or future value, taking into account the passage of time and an assumed rate of return and inflation.

umbrella insurance   Personal liability insurance protection that provides insurance beyond the underlying coverage of an individual's auto and homeowners insurance policies.

underinsured   An individual who has insufficient insurance to protect them from the full risk of a potential loss.

uninsured An individual who has no insurance or protection from risk of potential loss.

uninsurable An individual who, because of known health conditions, represents a level of risk that an insurance company is not willing to underwrite.

universal life insurance Flexible cash value life insurance that typically pays a current, competitive rate of interest on cash value accumulations. Universal life offers a variety of options that result in a flexible product design. At the policy owner's discretion, premium mode and amount can vary as well as death benefit options. Policy loans of cash value are available at an interest rate stipulated in the insurance contract. Partial withdrawals of cash value are also available.

unsecured debt Debt that is issued without collateral.

unsubsidized loans A loan that is not supported in any way by a federal agency or other third part. One example is one type of Stafford loan. This type of loan accrues (accumulates) interest while a student is in school, during the six-month grace period after leaving school, and during any authorized periods of deferment and forbearance. *See also* subsidized loans.

U.S. Savings Bonds Bonds that are issued by the U.S. Dept. of the Treasury and backed by the full faith and credit of the United States Government.

U.S. Treasury Securities Any debt instrument issued by the United States government. These include Treasury Bills, notes, and bonds.

The interest rates for federal (and many private) student loans are based on the results of Treasury Bill auctions held throughout the year by the U.S. government. Treasury Bills and other "securities" are sold to the public to pay off maturing government debt and to raise the cash needed to operate the federal government. *See also* T-bill.

variable universal life insurance Flexible cash value life insurance that offers a number of investment account options in addition to the other features of a universal life policy. *See also* universal life insurance.

Veteran's Administration (VA) Loans VA loans are available to qualifying individuals and families and carry slightly lower interest rates than are commercially available, with lower requirements for downpayments as well.

waiver of premium An insurance policy rider that waives the required premium payment in the event of an extended period of disability.

waiver of charges An insurance policy rider that waives the mortality charges of a life insurance policy during an extended period of disability.

waiting period Period of time between the onset of disability and the payment of benefits under the terms of the policy. *See also* elimination period.

whole life insurance A fixed life insurance policy for the life of the insured.

Index

T

U